THE ESSENTIAL SMALL BUSINESS GUIDE TO FINANCIAL MANAGEMENT

STREAMLINED STRATEGIES FOR MAXIMIZED PROFITS, COMPLIANCE, AND LONG-TERM SUCCESS FOR MONEY-STRESSED ENTREPRENEURS

DBR PUBLISHING

This book is dedicated to the entrepreneurs and small business owners of Northwest Arkansas. Thank you for all of your support and encouragement with special thanks to the parents of Dr. Bryan Raya, Sindi McGuire and Ernie Raya. It is a true blessing to have such amazing people in our lives!

FOREWORD

In the world of entrepreneurship, there's an exhilarating thrill that comes with turning your passion and vision into a thriving small business. However, as any business owner knows, this exhilaration can often be tempered by financial stress and uncertainty. That's where this book, "The Essential Small Business Guide to Financial Management," swoops in as a beacon of clarity, guidance, and hope.

I'm Dr. Bryan Raya, an entrepreneur just like you. My journey began with a passion for helping people succeed, which led me to establish a bookkeeping business, DBR Bookkeeping. As a former professor in higher education and a veteran of the U.S. Army, I felt that being just a bookkeeper wasn't enough to help my fellow entrepreneurs. Soon I began hosting the "Doing

Business Right" podcast to share the stories and insights of entrepreneurs with others in the small business community. I've had the privilege of meeting countless remarkable entrepreneurs, each with a unique story, ambition, and dream. A common struggle I see, and what unites us all, is the recognition that navigating the financial intricacies of our businesses can be a complex and overwhelming task.

Enter this book, a comprehensive and invaluable resource crafted by experts in the field. I didn't want to create just another financial management manual; but a guide with specific strategies to help entrepreneurs on the path to sustainable success. I've selected the following themes in this guide as I felt these were the biggest stresses I heard from business owners of all sizes and industries - profits, compliance, and long-term stability.

"The Essential Small Business Guide to Financial Management" doesn't just stop at imparting knowledge; it empowers you to take control of your financial destiny. Whether you're a seasoned entrepreneur or just beginning your journey, the strategies within these pages are designed to streamline your financial processes, maximize your profits, and provide you with the peace of mind that comes from knowing your business is on a secure financial footing.

As you embark on your entrepreneurial journey, remember that you're not alone. Thousands of entrepreneurs have walked this path before you, and countless more will follow in your footsteps. By embracing the wisdom within this book, you join a community of resilient and forward-thinking individuals dedicated to Doing Business Right.

So, my fellow entrepreneurs, let's dive into this essential guide together. Let's transform financial stress into financial success. Because, ultimately, the journey of entrepreneurship isn't just about profit; it's about the pursuit of a life well-lived through the businesses we build to help our communities and others. Welcome to a world where financial management becomes your superpower, and your entrepreneurial dreams become a reality.

To your success,
Dr. Bryan Raya
DBR Publishing
Doing Business Right

TABLE OF CONTENTS

INTRODUCTION

An entrepreneur's dreams emerge in droves, but many crumble as fast as they were dreamt up in the first place. You have to peek at the statistics regarding the U.S.'s new business failure rates to understand how tough it could be to build a thriving enterprise. Data from the U.S. Bureau of Labor Statistics (BLS) reveals that about 20% of newly established businesses collapse within their first years. At the same time, almost half of them don't celebrate their fifth birthdays. A prolonged existence doesn't guarantee survival since the new-business failure rate surges to about 65% in the first ten years (U.S. BLS, n.d.). These failure rates have stayed relatively consistent since 1994, when the BLS began collecting this data.

So, what do these failure rates mean? If 600,000 new businesses launch, 390,000 will be bankrupt before a decade lapse. Based on this data and how your business is doing, consider how you would answer the following questions:

- Are you concerned your business could be the next to fail in the coming years?
- Does your business lack the cash needed to cover its emergency expenses?
- Do you feel overwhelmed with the financial complexity and responsibility of running your small business?
- Does your company's expenses exceed its revenue?
- Do you have trouble *analyzing* your company's financial statements?

If you've answered yes to any of the above questions, you have a good reason to be concerned about the survival of your business. Let us explain.

Many entrepreneurs enter small businesses to be their own boss and carry out their ideas. Although they tend to have the expertise to turn their ideas into products and services, they often need more business skills, such as financial management and marketing. Thousands of entrepreneurs hire accountants to prepare financial statements, but they don't read and analyze them. It shouldn't be surprising that cash flow or lack of funding often pop up as reasons for business failures.

In a nutshell, business owners struggle because of the following factors:

- **Limited financial knowledge:** Small business owners struggle with concepts like budgeting, cash flow, and financial reporting.
- **Marketing challenges:** Entrepreneurs face difficulties developing effective advertising strategies to attract and retain customers.
- **Time management:** Small business owners often wear too many hats and thus lack time for strategic planning and growth.
- **Legal and compliance issues:** Understanding and complying with legal requirements, regulations, and tax obligations can overwhelm small business owners.
- **Scaling and growth:** Transitioning from a small startup to a sustainable and scalable business poses challenges, including identifying growth opportunities, accessing funding, and managing increasingly complex situations.

When faced with a combination of the challenges mentioned above, entrepreneurship ceases to excite—in fact, it sucks out your energy. Try to understand that it's not your fault that you have to deal with these challenges. Schools and our home lives rarely prepare us for the world of entrepreneurship. We're forced to learn as we go, and we're bound to make mistakes. Unfortunately, some of these mistakes make building and growing our businesses hard. Imagine how troublesome it'd be to run a small business facing mounting debt and struggling to make a profit!

Well, there's a way to minimize the mistakes you make as you build your business—and that is by learning from the mistakes that others have made. It's even better if you could learn these mistakes before you make them, which is precisely where this book on financial management comes in.

Financial management is a business function that plans, organizes, directs, and controls financial resources to nail your company's goals. It also plays a significant role in business decision-making. The critical financial management activities include budgeting, cash flow management, credit management, debt management, financial reporting and analysis, and creating financial projections. Effective financial management can be your gateway to business success! It will ensure you make data-driven decisions for the present and future, help secure financing, and create the foundation for your company's scalability and growth.

The output of the effort you put into your business's finances will be a financially stable company with predictable revenues, profits, and cash. In essence, here's what entrepreneurial success will look like once you've applied everything you've learned in this book:

- Your business will be **financially stable and profitable**, ensuring **long-term sustainability and growth**.
- You'll have a marketing strategy consistently delivering your **desired return on investment (ROI)**. When you want to increase the number of customers, you'll know what marketing channel, message, and content format to use.
- You'll know how to **streamline your operations, be effective**, and consistently **deliver your desired business results**.
- Your business will **comply with applicable laws and regulations** and **avoid legal risks and penalties**.
- Your business will expand and capitalize **on growth opportunities** such as entering new markets or broadening your product line.

Learning to manage your business's finances is part and parcel of turning your entrepreneurship dream into reality. That's why this book doesn't just focus on theories but provides actionable, tested strategies and tactics you can apply immediately in your business. Its simple, straightforward language simplifies complex financial concepts, making them easier to understand and use. If you thought understanding a business's finances is for accounting professionals only, you'd be wrong—and will be convinced soon enough.

Rest assured that investing time and effort into reading this comprehensive guide on financial management will be worth it. With this book's expertise instilled in your mind, you won't have to worry about the economic challenges you will likely face. Furthermore, you will know how to maximize profits and cost-effectively expand your business. Not only will you learn practical strategies and tactics to make your business profitable, but you'll also position your venture for long-term viability.

No matter how complex your financial worries are, this book will turn your confusion into clarity and your fear into confidence. This book is the guide that will walk with you, step-by-step, toward financial success. Now, without further ado, let's make your entrepreneurial dreams a reality!

1

THE POWER OF BUSINESS BUDGETING AND THE MANAGEMENT OF CASH FLOW AND CREDIT

I n the world of entrepreneurship, simple ideas can turn into brilliant businesses. Innovation and dreams alone aren't enough to create a successful business, and this is a harsh truth we can confront by looking at a study conducted by CB Insights (2021), a market intelligence platform. This study dissected 110 failed startups to decipher what led to their demise. Can you guess what it found? The foremost reason for the failure was running out of cash or not raising enough money in the first place.

You can have a groundbreaking business idea and not make it simply due to lack of cash. This issue can relate to poor business budgeting (or a total lack thereof). In this chapter, you'll discover how to create a business budget and manage cash flow and debt.

THE CRITICAL ROLE OF BUDGETING

When we mentioned that a budget can be the difference between running out of cash or failing to raise capital, you may have doubted us. After all, a business can only survive a couple of years without proper budgeting. And while this may be true, the chances of survival diminish with the passing of each year. The owner likely must keep financing their business to stay afloat. Entrepreneurs who want to be successful create a budget for their businesses. A case in point is the venture described below.

An agri-industrial company wanted a budget to determine where it could invest, establish operational priorities, and choose the best way to fund its business. Due to its strong management team, this business has seen double-digit growth for seven years. Its major challenge was that it depended on a single product susceptible to changing climatic conditions.

The company hired a financial services startup to closely examine its operations and guide it on how best to invest its funds and stay in the green. The budget unveiled areas the business could invest in and profit from through experimenting and examining several scenarios. While finding the optimum method of funding those investments was the primary aim, the budget analysis revealed financial benchmarks the company could use to gauge its future performance and the success of its assets. This long-term strategy was crucial for the long-term financial stability of the company.

At the core of the exercise mentioned above was a business budget. Without it, management would have made business decisions based on gut feeling alone. Emotions may be great for protecting us from harm, but they're weak masters when it comes to making financial decisions.

Why Do You Need a Business Budget?

Imagine you're a ship's captain and want to visit a place you've never been. What single tool will you need to ensure you get to your destination? If you guessed the navigation, then you're absolutely right! A well-thought-out budget is your business tool to navigate your entrepreneurial journey.

Simply put, your business budget keeps you on the path to your dream. Some of the benefits it'll give you include the following:

- **It forces you to set business goals.** Although a budget is flexible and allows you to change some goals, it helps keep yourself accountable to the original objectives you set. If you have to change, you'd need to devise genuine reasons, which might dissuade you from making goal changes often.

- **It facilitates making major financial decisions.** A proper budget will give you confidence when making big financial decisions. It can help you decide whether to make a particular investment or not.

- **It simplifies making tax estimates and preparation.** Proper budgeting should show what profits you're likely to make. This, in turn, simplifies the estimation and preparation of your company's taxes.

- **It prepares you for emergencies.** A business, like an individual, can be faced with the unexpected.

- **It shows what expenses your revenues should cover.** Your budget shows how efficient you are at converting the revenue into profit—how well you control expenses, to put it another way. The budget begins with knowing your expenses and how much each costs you.

If you closely check the above benefits of budgeting, you'll notice that each is about making your business prosper. For your business to be self-sufficient and thrive, it's worth creating and maintaining a budget. It's also crucial to review the budget against actual costs at regular intervals, including monthly, quarterly, and annually, for it to be effective. Before jumping to creating a budget, let's first explore the different kinds of business budgeting methods.

Five Business Budgeting Methods You Should Know About

Before you start creating a budget for your business, it's essential to understand the different budgeting methods. The few methods we'll discuss in this chapter are the following:

- zero-based budgeting
- activity-based budgeting
- flexible budgeting
- incremental budgeting
- value proposition budgeting

Don't worry, we'll simplify each method below to help you decide which suits your business best.

Zero-Based Budgeting

This is the method you use to develop your budget from scratch. It's ideally suited for a startup because it doesn't require a record of historical revenues and expenses. The zero-based budgeting (ZBB) method has pros and cons, of course, including the following:

- **Pros:** It produces a detailed budget and focuses on cost drivers—business activities directly linked with revenue. It prevents ballooning ongoing expenses related to your company's activities that aren't adding value now for established businesses.
- **Cons:** It's time-consuming and resource-intensive due to the extensive research needed. ZBB tends to focus more on the short term to meet current needs, which could negatively impact long-term goals.

An excellent example of ZBB is researching and finding that you can spend $1,000 on your supplies. This amount is the figure that you budget.

Activity-Based Budgeting

The most critical business activities to scrutinize are your expenses that likely prove most costly, such as payroll and job supplies. This analysis can also mean finding wasteful and inefficient areas for your business. The pros and cons of activity-based budgeting (ABB) include the following:

- **Pros:** ABB prevents spending money on noncore business activities by focusing on cost drivers. It also helps your business identify inefficiencies and eliminate them. This, in turn, reduces your costs and improves profits.
- **Cons:** It's resource-intensive due to the required analysis and research. ABB isn't ideal for you if you lack accounting skills and an intensive understanding of your business.

A good example of ABB is figuring out how much to budget to produce 20,000 burgers annually if you run a restaurant business. The number of burgers made per year is one of your cost drivers. Suppose that it costs your restaurant $6 to produce one burger. You'll need to budget $6 times 20,000, totaling $120,000 annually. You would repeat this same exercise for all your cost drivers to determine your total expenses for your period.

Flexible Budgeting

Use this method when revenues and expenses are inconsistent during the fiscal period. It's a hybrid budgeting method that incorporates the static and dynamic approaches. The pros and cons of flexible budgeting are as follows:

- **Pros:** Flexible budgeting allows easy running of "what if" scenarios for improved financial projections. It also matches reality in that business revenues and expenses rarely stay consistent from one period to the next.
- **Cons:** Flexible budgeting takes time to create and maintain, and it's not as accurate as the ABB method.

An example of flexible budgeting is when an unpredictable event requires adjusting revenues and expenses. For example, suppose you've planned to produce 60 items of your product during the last quarter of the year. Because each item sells for $10 and costs $2 to make, you can expect to generate $600 in revenue for $120. Let's say that an event occurs that you're sure will raise demand for your product to 90 items instead of 60. Your new expected revenue is $900, while the cost will be $180. Flexible budgeting will allow you to make these adjustments and maintain the accuracy of your budget. It also allows you to take opportunities and adjust your financial decisions when there's excess money.

Incremental Budgeting

This budgeting method involves making minor adjustments to the recent budget or actual revenues and expenses to prepare a new budget. The pros and cons of incremental budgeting include the following:

- **Pros:** It's a simple budgeting method that a non-accounting or inexperienced person can use. Incremental budgeting ensures that long-term projects stay funded.
- **Cons:** It's easy to keep historical costs unrelated to your revenue in your budget, which can take money away from core business activities. Incremental budgeting makes minor changes to a past budget, which may be inaccurate if more money is needed. In short, incremental budgeting isn't suitable for new businesses.

A good example of incremental budgeting is when you want to determine next year's marketing budget. If the actual marketing spent during the previous year was $10,000, you can increase 10% to this figure to budget for this year.

Value Proposition Budgeting

With this method, you analyze and explain your business's expenses and revenue to ensure you spend money where it's valuable to do so. Put simply, it seeks to find meaning behind each cost. While value is subjective, you can define what it means for your business. The pros and cons of value proposition budgeting (VPB) include the following:

- **Pros:** VPB allows you to determine where each dollar of revenue goes and why it goes there. It's an excellent method when you want to prioritize expenses. This method eliminates wasteful expenditure since it focuses on costs that bring the most value to your business.
- **Cons:** Defining value can be tricky, which makes VPB challenging to get right. Like ZBB and ABB, VPB is time-consuming.

A good example of value proposition budgeting is when a business defines its target audience, researches the competition, and determines its value proposition. Suppose your company finds that your target audience values customer service more than anything else. Based on this, you allocate funds to deliver the best customer experience from your website to product delivery and follow-ups.

Now that you've seen these budgeting methods think about your business and how it operates, and decide which approach works best for you. In your assessment, ask yourself questions like the ones below and make sure you've figured out the answer:

- Is my business a startup with no annual records of actual expenses? If so, perhaps a zero-based or activity-based budget would suit you.
- Does my business generate consistent revenues and expenses year in and year out? Maybe ZBB, ABB, incremental budgeting, or VPB is your go-to method.
- Is my business seasonal, generating inconsistent and sporadic revenues and expenses? If so, perhaps the flexible budgeting method suits you better.
- Does my business want to focus on delivering value to its target audience? Maybe VPB is your go-to budgeting method.

Challenge yourself to come up with other questions to help you select your best budgeting method. Consider factors such as complexity, accounting knowledge, business acumen, and other factors when thinking about this.

Now that you know what budgeting method would be the best fit for your business, let's discover how to create an effective budget.

Practical Steps to Create and Manage a Business Budget

Get ready to discover the world of business budget-making and managing your business's financial affairs. Suppose you've been running your business for at least a year. In that case, you can take advantage of past years' data to unlock your budgeting process unless you prefer the ZBB method. For startup visionaries, your best bet is to use your research skills to uncover the essential information you need.

Since creating a business budget is a process, it's worth knowing the steps involved. Fasten your seat belts as this section unfolds and details each step of your business budgeting voyage. Before you execute the first step below, choose the kind of budgeting method suitable for your business needs. Let's kick-start this journey with the first step.

Figure Out Your Business Goals

Business goals are the targets you want to achieve by the end of a predetermined period, such as a year.

Every successful business has goals, and it's vital to have them if you want your company to outperform your competitors.

For a new business, one of your business goals could be to generate $50,000 in sales in the next 12 months. Older companies may have goals such as "To increase our net profit margin by 20% this year." Of course, it costs money to achieve business goals like these. For example, you'll need to spend more on certain costs, such as marketing and advertising, to increase your net profit. There should be no guesswork as to what those costs are and how much more you'll need to allocate them.

Estimate Your Annual Sales

The second step for creating a budget is estimating your annual sales. Business sales are also called revenue or income. How you estimate these sales depends on whether your business is new or already well-established.

In the case of an established business, you can base your current sales on the previous year's performance. For instance, if you made $100,000 in sales, you could increase them by 15% to $115,000 this year.

If you're a startup, a great kick-off point is determining how many items (products or services) you expect to sell and at what price. You can estimate the price and number of items you'll sell from the industry research you perform before starting your business. Multiply the number of items by the price of each item to arrive at total sales. For instance, if you sell 3,000 items at $2,000 apiece a year, your total annual sales is $6 million.

Analyze Your Annual Costs

Regardless of the budgeting method you prefer, initiating that method will involve understanding what costs you're bound to incur in running your business. Having all the information you need will improve the accuracy of your budget, which will help ensure you achieve your business and financial goals.

There are two major categories of costs to factor into your budget:

- **Fixed costs:** These expenses stay constant irrespective of the revenues you generate. Examples include accounting software subscriptions, accounting services, salary, and rent.
- **Variable costs:** These are costs that vary based on the level of revenue you make. Examples of variable costs include sales commissions, shipping fees, and production supplies.

In researching your business's expenses, find out what percentage of your revenue goes to each category of costs. Major business expenses vary by industry and type of company. Your typical significant costs as percentages of revenue are as follows:

- Payroll: 15%–30% (Holliday, 2020)
- Marketing: 5%–25% (BrightEdge, n.d.)
- Rent: 2%–20% (Sherman, 2019)
- Taxes: 30% (Barton, 2022)
- Emergency fund: 10%–30% (Grunden, 2020)

Some of the sources for your research will include your cost records, industry average costs, and the Internal Revenue Service (IRS) website. You can work out your profit when you've gathered all the expected costs.

Tip: Brace for the unexpected by setting aside a percentage of your revenues for emergencies. Who knows when bad luck might sneak up and leave your bank account dry?

Adjust the Above to a Monthly Budget

A business budget works well, provided you review it regularly to make timely adjustments. Conducting such reviews each month is reasonable as this period offers enough time to make adjustments necessary to achieve your business goals.

To adjust the above budget into a monthly one, divide the annual dollar figures by 12. For instance, if your annual revenue is $120,000, your monthly revenues will each be $12,000 on average. Note that some months' actual revenues might be higher than the average while others are lower. These variations are acceptable so long as your annual average is as planned.

And there you have it: That's all there is to creating a business budget. Again, you first decide what budgeting method to use before making your budget. Business budgeting requires setting business goals, estimating sales, researching costs, and adjusting your annual budget to a monthly one. Remember to keep your budgeting process simple, especially if you're a new business owner.

Why You Should Track Your Business's Income and Expenses

Envision your business standing tall among its peers. That achievement will stay a dream unless you create a budget and commit to tracking your income and expenses. As entrepreneurs, we usually don't feel too excited about handling our businesses' finances. But this lack of excitement can put our businesses at risk of collapsing due to lack of cash. Tracking your business's income and expenses helps solve this problem and delivers some compelling rewards, as discussed below:

- **You can save taxes.** Many business expenses can reduce your taxable income and increase your profit. You'll need to record and track all your expenses to deduct them for tax purposes.
- **You'll be ready with documents needed for filing taxes, applying for finance, or an IRS audit.** Tracking income and expenses allows you to maintain organized finances.
- **You'll improve your financial planning.** As noted earlier, past revenues and expenses can feed into your future budget, depending on your budgeting method. Tracking your revenues and expenses—and ensuring they're accurate—will help create accurate financial plans. You'll also make timely adjustments to prevent overspending and stay on course to nailing your business goals.
- **You'll spot opportunities to cut unnecessary costs.** When you know where you're spending money, you can determine whether some of those costs add value.
- **You can identify fraud quickly.** Fraud can happen in your business both internally and externally. You can soon spot embezzlement and protect your funds when you track expenses.

- **You can determine the profitability of your business.** Tracking your business's expenses and revenues will help you calculate its profits or losses. This tracking will enable you to decide how to achieve your desired profits.

A critical expense to monitor is the cost of goods sold (COGS), which refers to the costs directly tied to manufacturing your product or creating your service. Other key expenses to look out for are payroll, rent, marketing and advertising, taxes, and interest. When tracking these expenses and revenues, compare them with your budget estimates, as this will ensure you stay on the path to achieving your business goals. If you realize at any point that you've strayed from the course, you can adjust your business before it's too late.

You'd agree that budgeting and tracking your expenses can be the difference between winning and losing in business. While you're likely still excited about the benefits of tracking your expenses, why not readily learn how to do it?

Three Steps to Track Your Business Expenses

Proper business tracking begins with having meticulous financial records. The value of these records will show up when you need them, such as when reviewing your budget. Safeguard your documents in almost the same manner as a lion guards its territory. This idea leads us to the three steps we recommend you follow to track your business costs properly.

- **Step 1: Open a business account and credit card.** It's common for entrepreneurs and small business owners to combine their personal finances with their businesses. While this may feel like simplifying your personal and business finances, it complicates them. It's hard to know which expenses and incomes are for your business and which aren't. The solution is to open a business account and a business credit card.

- **Step 2: Keep your paper and digital receipts safe.** You can't claim tax deductions without proof of qualifying business expenses. Receipts, whether paper or digital, serve this function. Paper receipts can be cumbersome to store safely. Your best bet is to scan and file them in computer folders dedicated to each month of expenses. You can place digital receipts in the same folders.

- **Step 3: Use an expense-tracking tool.** Manually tracking expenses and comparing them with your budget can be challenging. You should most likely use some accounting software to organize your expenses for easier reviewing against the budget. This software can automatically record expenses and revenues because it can connect to your business's bank accounts. Choose accounting software based on your business's life stage.

As we'll discuss next, tracking your income and expenses also feeds into your future budgeting and forecasting.

How to Improve Your Budgeting and Forecasting

No budget or forecast accurately estimates what will happen in the future. Yet, having a budget and a forecast is essential for keeping your business on the right path. For your budget and forecast to closely match reality, you must keep adjusting and improving your budgets and forecasts over time. Here are some of the ways you can ensure this happens:

- **Create rolling budgets and forecasts.** This will allow you to factor in actual expenses and incomes, making your budgets and forecasts more accurate. Also, you'll adjust your numbers based on the changes you think will affect your previous budget and forecast.

- **Make flexible budgets and forecasts.** Adjust your budgets and forecasts as and when you deem necessary. Business conditions change, and you can't base your decisions on outdated factors.
- **Clarify your business goals before budgeting and forecasting.** Your budgets and forecasts should enable you to achieve your business goals. Setting and clarifying these goals is essential to align with your budgets and forecasts.

Failure to create a business budget and track your expenses will lead to your business's downfall. Consider how and when you will track your business's expenses to avoid this. Resolve to follow through with your expense-tracking plan, and you'll be sure to always have money in the bank. Speaking of money in the bank, the next section will dissect a vital concept that trips up all kinds of business owners with brilliant business ideas.

UNDERSTANDING AND MANAGING CASH FLOW

You've likely heard the adage, "Cash is king." It may sound cliché, but nowhere is this truth more evident than in small businesses. Remember the primary reason CB Insights discovered was behind the demise of 110 startups it dissected? It wasn't a lack of revenues—it was a cash shortage. What could be the issue if a small business generates sales but crashes due to insufficient funds? Well, it boils down to an improper use of cash, leading to a misunderstanding of cash flow. Don't get too flustered by this concept if you're unfamiliar. This section will delve deeper into cash flow.

What Is Cash Flow and Why Is It Important?

Cash is what lubricates the gears that make your business work. A business with zero or negative cash flow signifies a venture like a car with no oil. If you don't address the problem, the car locks up and stops working. If you look away for an extended period, it may sadly die. It's crucial to prevent your business from getting into such a state by understanding how to manage cash flow. Before exploring how to manage your business's cash flow, let's first go over why cash flow is vital for your business.

- **It helps you decide when to expand.**
  Expanding when your business's cash flow is positive and significant is a good idea.
- **It improves your business's financial planning.** Understanding your cash flow with

other business metrics allows for better financial management. This way, you sidestep the likelihood of making costly business and financial errors.

- **It makes your business look intriguing to investors.** We have no way of knowing what your business's exit strategy is. If you intend to sell it at some point, it'll be easier if your business is cash-rich.
- **It helps prevent expense mismanagement.** Failure to watch your cash flow will let unnecessary expenses slip through the cracks and hemorrhage cash out of your business.

There's no doubt that cash flow is a vital component of a successful business. More importantly, closely watching it will help you channel your business in the right direction. Furthermore, as discussed next, monitoring your cash flow will help you distinguish it from your business's profit.

Cash Flow vs Profit

Cash flow and profit measure the amount of money coming into your business. They are, however, unique from one another. It's possible for your business to make a profit but have no cash to pay its suppliers. This concept can be tricky and confusing to many entrepreneurs. Understanding the difference between cash flow and profit will help you use each of these metrics for their intended purposes.

You've already learned that cash flow is about how much cash you have. In contrast, profit tells you how much of your revenue remains after paying all expenses over a given reporting period, such as a year.

This money forms part of the cash flow over the same period. Like cash flow, profit can be negative, zero, or positive, and it's preferable to have a positive profit. Let's investigate the difference between cash flow and profit with a simple example.

Suppose that the ABC Company sells microwaves directly to customers for cash. It sells five microwaves during August in a particular year for $200 per item. The total revenue generated from the sales is $1,000. During the month, the company's total expenses are $850, meaning its profit is $150. In the same month, the company receives $100 in dividends and invests $50 in stocks.

The ABC Company's profit in August was $150. Its cash flow is $200 ($150 plus $100 minus $50), assuming it started the month with zero cash. You can see from this example that profit and cash flow are different. They can be equal in a specific month or year purely by coincidence. You'll learn more about cash flow and profit in the next chapter.

The bottom line is that cash flow and profit are essential metrics for any business. They serve different purposes and should be evaluated differently. The main takeaway is that cash flow isn't profit and vice versa. With this confusion clarified, let's now focus on cash flow management.

Five Practical Strategies for Managing Cash Flow

Cash flow management is the process of making sure that your business always has cash to meet its needs. To help keep your budget honest, monitor, analyze, and optimize incoming and outgoing funds to maximize cash flow. You can carry out this key task in numerous ways, including the following:

- **Invoicing customers quickly.** Your business needs to be paid as quickly as possible. If it doesn't deal with cash purchases, invoice your customers as soon as you finish the work agreed upon. Even if your customer pays you 30 or 60 days after receiving the invoice, quickly invoicing your customers can bring in cash faster.

- **Following up on due invoices.** You'd be surprised how many customers delay paying invoices even if they receive them on time. Others wait for you to make follow-ups before they process and pay your invoice. In addition to invoicing quickly, send reminders 10, 5, and 1 day before the invoice is due. If you institute interest or late fees, be sure those are clear at the time of invoicing and properly stated. Make follow-ups on the first day and regular intervals after the invoice is overdue.
- **Keeping a rainy day fund.** When your business produces excess cash, stash away some of it for unexpected events. Despite your efforts to invoice quickly and make follow-ups, emergencies can happen. For instance, you might land an opportunity that needs money soon while you have no cash. It may be gone for good if you don't have money to fund the opportunity. Sometimes, you'll need cash quickly to handle difficult times.

- **Paying bills just before they're due.** If you buy a service or product on credit, don't rush to pay the bill as soon as you receive it. Wait until it's about due before paying it. This delay ensures that you keep cash for as long as possible, and you might also earn a bit of interest from it. Some bills can be paid a few days after they're due without incurring late fees or penalties. If you have such bills, pay them as late as is allowable.
- **Keeping detailed financial records.** You don't only need financial records for filing taxes or IRS audits. Financial records enable you to keep tabs on your cash flow. Keep a trail of the bills you receive and schedule payment dates. You should have a similar record for invoices you've issued to your customers.

Having strategies for managing cash flow is great, but it's even better to know which ones are working and which aren't. If a process doesn't work well, discard it and try another. Your aim is to keep as much cash as possible in your pocket. The above methods of preserving your cash flow will make a positive difference to your business, even if you have debt—a topic we will discuss next.

AN OVERVIEW OF CREDIT MANAGEMENT

Does your business extend credit to your customers? Does your company buy products or services on credit? You need credit management if you said yes to either of these questions. Failure to expertly manage your customers' credit or your debt will jeopardize the chances of your business's survival. Before learning the ins and outs of credit management, you should know its importance.

What Is Credit Management and Why Is It Important?

Just as it is for an existing business, access to cash is paramount for launching a new one. As small businesses increase, more U.S. citizens become employed, reducing the unemployment rate. In turn, this improves the viability of small businesses due to the improved economy. This access to credit by small businesses may be dampened due to the surge in credit delinquencies (Snitkof, 2023). In response, lenders might tighten their lending criteria, depriving deserving entrepreneurial endeavors of opportunities to thrive.

You can differentiate your venture with effective credit management—ensuring that debts are paid on time whether you—or your customers—bought on credit. Every business that extends or buys on credit is responsible for ensuring that credit doesn't go out of hand. By now, you know the risk of survival if your customers don't pay you on time. Your suppliers also face the same risk, which may threaten your business's survival.

You effectively grant your customer a loan when you sell a product or service on credit. Unlike bank loans, you don't earn interest on the loans you extend. The risk you take when selling on credit can't be overlooked. You need effective credit management if you can't always sell for cash. When implemented, such management will deliver benefits such as the following:

- **Protection of your business's financial stability:** Unpaid invoices reduce your cash and may threaten the survival of your business. Effective credit management helps you get paid, which stabilizes your finances.
- **Optimization of cash flow:** Strong credit management ensures you manage cash inflows and outflows effectively. Not only do you pay bills on time, but you also get paid on time. You can use the cash inflow for profitable business activities when paid on time. These payments ensure you keep optimal cash flow when coupled with making timely payments because you won't have to pay interest or penalties on overdue invoices.

- **Minimization or elimination of extra costs of credit:** When you pay late, your vendors may charge you penalties and interests. These charges will reduce your potential profits. When your customers pay their invoices late, you must chase them, which costs money and time. With proper credit management, you'll minimize these extra costs and optimize your business's cash.

- **Enhanced reputation in your industry:** Paying bills on time keeps your business in your suppliers' good books. Such a reputation can be helpful when you need cash during difficult times. Many suppliers will be eager to help because they know you tend to keep your word. Your business can also be an example to your customers in handling debt. These habits may influence them to ensure they pay your invoices on time.

- **Building strong relationships with suppliers and customers:** Relationships are priceless in business. Your suppliers and customers may help you when you face tough financial times. You can forge such relationships with proper credit management.

Look at how you currently handle credit and ask yourself, "How well is my credit management working?" Managing your business credit is crucial to your business's success. Confidence in your decisions requires a basic understanding of the types of business credit and how they affect your business. Next, we'll explore the basic types of business credit that apply to any industry.

Three Types of Business Credit

What do you do as a business owner when your venture faces a cash crunch? Perhaps despite your best efforts, multiple customers haven't paid their invoices, or you face an unexpected event that dries up your cash reserves. Before you dismiss this as hogwash, consider that 54% of small businesses across the U.S. battled with inconsistent cash flow and paying operational expenses (Fed Small Business, 2023).

Facing either of these scenarios, do you shut the doors of your business for good, or do you find ways to access some funds? Knowing your entrepreneurial spirit, you'll probably seek funds elsewhere. The likely source of funds to keep your business alive is business credit, whether a line of credit, a business loan, or charging the funds on your business credit card. Here's how these three work:

Business Line of Credit

A business line of credit is a traditional form of business funding that works like a credit card. Your business gets approved for funding up to a specific limit, and it's charged interest only on the portion it uses. When you repay, you can later access the same funds and pay them back with interest. This kind of credit is called a revolving credit facility.

Your business can use this money for various purposes, including buying inventory, paying invoices, or paying employee salaries.

A business line of credit can be secured or unsecured. The secured version requires collateral such as real estate or customer invoices for approval. For this reason, such lines of credit offer higher credit limits and charge lower interest rates. In contrast, an unsecured business line of credit doesn't require collateral to be approved. These factors make you more likely to be approved with lower credit limits and interest rates.

Like most types of funding, you'll be required to pay an origination, monthly, and annual fee for the privilege of having a business line of credit.

Business Loan

This general term refers to any commercial funding available from credit unions, traditional banks, and online lenders. You can use a business loan to fund business activities such as buying real estate, covering operating expenses, or purchasing equipment.

The typical business loan provides a lump sum to be repaid with interest and fees. Unlike a business line of credit, a business loan doesn't allow reusing. The most popular form of business loan is the term loan, which is a loan of a certain sum that must be repaid over a fixed period.

Business Credit Card

A business credit card is a revolving credit facility that works similarly to a personal credit card and business line of credit. The credit limit on this credit card is higher than on a personal credit card and gives you access to more rewards.

Use this credit card for business activities only. Don't try to use it for personal reasons because it comes with expense monitoring. Additionally, a business credit card provides business tools to enable the better running of your company.

Again, those are the three types of funding you could access when you need cash quickly. It's a good idea to be proactive and have one or two funding sources before you need them. However, remember that debt can be risky and requires effective management. If you mismanage it, you can easily mar your business credit score (briefly discussed below).

Business Credit Score

Just as there's a personal credit score, your business has a credit score—a number lenders use to measure your business's creditworthiness. Lenders use your business's credit score to decide on funding and credit approval.

The three major providers of credit scores are Dun & Bradstreet, Experian, and Equifax. Each of these business credit bureaus offers three types of business credit scores. Let's illustrate the meanings of the Dun & Bradstreet business credit scores.

Now, Dun & Bradstreet provides the paydex, failure, and delinquency scores. A paydex score ranges from 1 to 100, indicating the likelihood of a business making late payments. A high score is favorable as it means you will likely pay your debts on time. The lower this score is, the more likely your business is to pay its debt late. The delinquency score measures your business's likelihood of making late payments by 91 or more days or folds. It ranges from 1 to 5, with a high score being unfavorable and indicating that you have a high chance of making late payments or going bankrupt. The failure score indicates the likelihood of your business shutting its doors within the following year. It ranges from 1,001 to 1,875, with a higher score being favorable, as it means your business will likely survive the next 12 months.

If your business is likely to seek credit, its paydex and failure scores need to be high while its delinquency scores are low. Not only will this improve your chances of getting credit, but it'll also position you to get the following:

- Favorable business insurance rates
- Better supplier credit terms
- Lower business loan interest rates and other credit terms

Can you imagine what a catastrophe it'd be if you needed credit and couldn't get it? We wouldn't wish this to happen to anyone, especially business owners and entrepreneurs. You need trusted and proven methods to maintain your business credit in sharp shooting conditions. That way, you'll be confident of getting business credit when needed and at favorable terms. Here are four practical methods for keeping your business credit record clean:

- **Maintain old business credit cards.** An old business credit means you have an old credit account and signals that your business is financially responsible. A long business credit history contributes significantly to your business's credit score. Eliminating old credit cards wipes out that record. It will reduce your credit score and prevent you from getting business credit or credit on desirable terms. Keep old business credit cards for as long as possible.
- **Use less than 30% of your total credit limit.** The amount of business credit you use relative to the total available credit limit is called credit utilization. A good practice is using less than 30% of your total credit limit (Revenued, 2023). Make it a habit to repay all the credit you've used before making more withdrawals.
- **Pay your lenders on time.** This is as true for personal credit as it is for business credit. Paying lenders late decreases your business's credit score and may lead to disapproval of credit applications. It's wise to schedule these

payments closer to their due date to improve cash flow and your business's credit record.

- **Review your business's credit record regularly.** Ensuring your business's credit record is accurate is in your interest. Things like fraud could tarnish your credit record. If you don't regularly check your business's credit record, you may wake up one day to find it impaired. Sadly, you might not qualify for new credit, landing your business in trouble.

Practicing the above methods will help you maintain a clean business credit record. When you need credit on short notice, you'll know that you can likely find it and keep your entrepreneurship dreams alive. We encourage entrepreneurs to create good habits early in their business journey to help establish long-term stability and success.

DEBT MANAGEMENT

There's no guarantee in business that things will always go according to plan. Even if something proceeds as planned, you can't know when natural disasters and other adverse events may occur. When your business faces such circumstances, you may be forced into debt to keep it afloat. You may have to go into debt deeper if you're already in debt. This is where debt management comes in handy—gaining control over your debt.

When you face debt repayment difficulties, you have options you can gravitate toward, including the following:

- **Sell more of your products or services.** This is one of the quickest ways to generate more money and pay your debt. You can market your products or services more and acquire more customers. Alternatively, you can sell some of your products or services to customers who haven't bought them. Sometimes, you don't even need to sell more but increase your prices slightly, especially if your current prices are low.

- **Negotiate payment terms.** Your creditors know that any business can fall on hard times. Speak to yours and be upfront about your difficulties and the plan you have to pay them in full. They know it's in their best interest to assist you in paying them. They may grant you favorable payment terms, such as extending your repayment period. These negotiations will reduce your repayment amounts, making them affordable.

- **Refinance your debt.** Refinancing means you apply for a new loan with more favorable terms and pay off the older debt. Considering if you have a good business credit record and interest rates are low is a good idea.
- **Consolidate your business loans.** Do you have loans or debt with multiple creditors? If so, consider consolidating those loans into one. Although the balance won't decline, you'll save on interest payments, which may be enough to give you some breathing space. To make this strategy more effective, negotiate lower interest rates.
- **Cut business expenses.** This is another quick way to get some control over your debt repayments. Look for ways to cut business expenses without decreasing your revenue and profits. Some cost-cutting methods include reducing inventory, doing some of the outsourced work yourself, negotiating decreased working hours for noncritical employees, and communication costs. Here's a quick warning: Avoid slashing marketing costs because you'll dry up your business's revenue and worsen the situation.

Our credit management and debt management discussion concluded by covering tools that form the foundation of a successful small business. You've now seen how crucial budgeting and cash flow are to the survival and success of a business. So, have you thought about what kind of budgeting method works for your business? What plans do you have in place to maintain a positive cash flow? Think about some reasons as to why your business needs to maintain a good credit record and note them down. Also, identify a couple of ideas you can use to keep your business's debt under control.

The solid foundation you've set during this chapter simplifies financial reporting—a means to facilitate informed financial and nonfinancial decision-making and enhanced business transparency. Understanding financial reporting takes your financial management skills to a higher level, and you can find out more about this in the next chapter.

2

TRANSPARENCY AND FINANCIAL REPORTING

Imagine crafting an accurate business budget and realizing you'll be cash-poor before reaching your goal! On top of that, you also know that if you don't attain this goal, your business's collapse is all but inevitable. What's the solution? Well, one way is to apply for business credit. Can you guess what lenders will want to see? Your business's financial reports, of course! This makes it imperative to understand the art and science of financial reporting, which this chapter is about, and offer many more insights.

WHY FINANCIAL REPORTING MATTERS

If you doubt the importance of financial reports, also called financial statements, the following case study will get you thinking twice:

In 2012, the University of Florida's Small Business Development Center (SBDC) consulted with 14 expansion-driven small businesses. These businesses spanned ten industries and had been operating for three years or longer. Before providing any assistance, the SBCD scrutinized the financial performances of each of these firms. Additionally, it surveyed the business owners to gauge their level of business financial knowledge. The primary aim was to determine if a small business's financial performance and its owner's business financial knowledge correlated.

Of the small businesses evaluated, 92.9% of them prepared financial reports. Yet, half of the companies examined had financial troubles. It turned out that 85.7% of the owners of businesses with financial problems didn't review and analyze their company's financial reports. The SBCD had no choice but to conclude that a small business's economic strength is heavily associated with its financial performance.

Unsurprisingly, all the business owners of small businesses facing financial stress admitted that they didn't understand business finances (Dahmen & Rodríguez, 2014). The major takeaway from the above case study is that you must understand business finances. With that knowledge, you'll have every reason to review and analyze your business's financial reports. With that said, let's move on with learning business finance by understanding financial reporting.

Financial Reporting and Its Benefits

Financial reporting is a business activity that discloses your company's financial information and performance for a given decision-making period. The key word in that definition is "decision-making"—something small businesses that faced financial difficulties in the case study above couldn't do. The primary role of financial reporting is establishing how much money you generate, where this money goes, and how much remains in your business; financial reporting is about determining the financial health of your business.

Your financial reports are essential to examine your business's financial affairs and comply with the law. When you have accurate finance reports, here's how you and your business will benefit:

- **You'll make improved financial decisions.**
  Financial reports reveal the performance of

your business over a given period. When analyzed over multiple periods, you'll identify trends and be able to estimate what may happen in the near future. For instance, the movements may show that your business is becoming overindebted. With this information, you get to decide the best course of action in the future. If you want to expand your business, financial reports will provide insight into the best time.

- **It'll be simpler to raise capital.** We discussed business credit as a potential source of cash in the previous chapter. Lenders won't consider your business credit application without financial reports. The reason is that financial statements show how creditworthy your business is. Private investors, family, and friends, also look at financial reports when deciding to invest in your business; this is where financial transparency comes in handy. Accurate financial statements will simplify the whole process of raising funds for business purposes.
- **You'll better plan your business's income taxes.** Your financial reports calculate how much corporate tax you'll pay over a period.

Understanding this, you can plan your business's cash flow to optimize the money that remains in your business after paying taxes. Because of the effort expended in creating financial reports, you'll minimize errors and save time during the tax season; using this time can maximize your business's cash flow or improve operations.

- **Your business will comply with the law.** Companies must prepare financial reports for tax purposes. Financial statements ensure that you stay in the good books of the law.

Consider the importance of financial reporting and ask yourself how it could help your business based on where it is today. It doesn't matter whether your business's finances are in good shape; there are one or two things financial reporting can help you accomplish. Let's take this to another level and examine the kinds of financial reports you have in your business.

COMPONENTS AND TYPES OF FINANCIAL REPORTS

The main types of financial reports are the income statement, balance sheet, and cash flow statement.

Don't fret if you're unfamiliar with these financial statements; we'll discuss each shortly. Each financial statement has components that make it unique from others. Financial reports must be audited by finance professionals such as accountants for accuracy when used for official purposes such as taxes.

Income Statement

An income statement also called the profit and loss statement, is a finance report that states a business's revenue, expenses, and profit (or loss). The primary purpose of the income statement is to report a company's profitability. Its main components include the following:

- **Revenue:** A business's total income for selling its products or services. This kind of income is called operating revenue. Some businesses also include income from non-core activities, such as rental property income, as part of their revenues.
- **Expenses:** These include the costs the business incurs to generate revenue and costs that directly support activities in producing the services or products sold. The costs linked directly with the production of sold goods or services are called the cost of goods sold

(COGS). Necessary supportive costs, called overheads, included in the income statement are a) research and development, b) selling, general and administrative expenses (SG&A), and c) salaries. Other expenses such as depreciation and amortization, interest paid on debt, and losses made from sales of assets are included here.

- **Depreciation:** This refers to the loss in value of a physical asset such as a truck. A specific cost gets allocated to this expense over the useful life of a tangible asset.

- **Amortization:** This is similar to depreciation except that it's applied to an intangible asset you buy, such as a trademark.

- **Gross profit:** This is when you subtract COGS from total revenue. For instance, a business with $20,000 in total revenue and $8,000 in COGS has a gross profit of $12,000 ($20,000 − $8,000 = $12,000). When you divide this $12,000 by the $20,000 of revenue, you get 60% if you express the result as a percentage. This metric, called the gross margin, measures how well direct business activities perform to bring in revenue. The higher it is, the better the productivity of your business.

- **Operating profit:** This is also called earnings before tax, interest, and amortization (EBITDA), and it's the profit realized when you subtract overheads from the gross profit. For instance, if your gross profit is $12,000 and overheads are $7,000, your operating profit is $5,000 ($12,000 — $7,000 = $5,000). You can also express it as a percentage of the total revenue to determine the operating profit margin. For example, a business with $5,000 in operating profit and $20,000 in total revenue has an operating profit margin of 25% ($5,000/$20,000 x 100 = 0.25 x 100 = 25%). You want your operating profit to be as high as possible.

- **Earnings before taxes:** This is the profit you make after subtracting depreciation, amortization, and interest from your operating profit, meaning earnings before taxes = operating profit – depreciation — amortization – interest. For example, suppose a business has $200 in depreciation, $130 in amortization, $350 in interest payment, and $5,000 in operating profit. In that case, its earnings before taxes will be $4,230 ($5,000 – $200 – $130 – $350 = $4,230). Your company's income tax is calculated based on this component.

- **Net profit or loss:** This component is also known as the bottom line because it usually occurs at the end of an income statement. You obtain it by subtracting taxes from your earnings before taxes figure. For instance, at a 21% tax rate, a business with $4,230 in earnings before tax will pay $888.30 ($4,230 x 21% = $888.30) in income taxes. Its net profit (earnings before taxes – taxes) will be $3,341.70 ($4,230 – $888.30 = $3,341.70.

It's easier to understand the above components when they appear in an income statement. Check them out in the example income statement below for a hypothetical company, here named PXZ, LLC:

PXZ, LLC

Date: 1 March 2023
Income Statement

	2023 Current year
Revenue	
Gross sales	$100,000.00
Less: sales returns	$5,000.00
Net Sales	**$95,000.00**
Cost of Goods Sold	
Goods manufactured: Raw materials	$20,000.00
Goods manufactured: Direct labor	$30,000.00
Total Cost of Goods Sold	$50,000.00
Gross Profit (Loss)	**$45,000.00**
Operating Expenses	
Delivery/freight expense	$5,000.00
Depreciation	$500.00
Insurance	$1,000.00
Mileage	$1,500.00
Office supplies	$1,000.00
Travel	$1,500.00
Utilities/telephone expenses	$2,500.00
Wages	$12,000.00
Other expenses	$500.00
Total Operating Expenses	$25,500.00
Operating Profit (Loss)	**$19,500.00**
Interest income	$0.00
Other income	$0.00
Profit Before Taxes	**$19,500.00**
Less: tax expense	$4,095.00
Net Profit (Loss)	**$15,405.00**

If PXY is cash-based, it should have added $15,405 to its bank account during the past year.

On its own, the income statement isn't beneficial. You'll need to compare its components with the corresponding metrics in your budget and the previous similar period. The reason is to gauge whether your business has delivered according to plan or is improving.

Balance Sheet

This financial report primarily displays two things: what your business owns and what it owes. The things that your company owns are assets, while what it owes are called liabilities. The main components of a balance sheet include the following:

- **Assets:** This component is broken down into short-term assets and long-term assets, also called capital assets. Short-term assets include cash and assets that can turn into cash within one year, such as inventory, treasury bills, and certificates of deposits (CDs). Long-term assets take more than a year to convert them into cash. Examples of capital assets include equipment, trademarks, and real estate property.

- **Liabilities:** Like assets, liabilities can be short-term or long-term. Short-term liabilities include bills for services rendered or products bought, loan repayments, and invoices such as commitments to purchase raw materials. Long-term liabilities are to be settled over more than one year and include mortgages and other loans to be repaid in more than a year.

- **Equity:** This is also called stockholders' or shareholders' equity—your business's net worth. For this book, we'll be referring to equity as shareholders' equity. You obtain it by subtracting total liabilities from total assets, meaning that total assets equals equity plus total liabilities (assets = liabilities + equity). If your business were to go bankrupt and pay all its debt, you would get the money captured as equity. Within equity sits a portion of net profits unpaid to business owners, called retained earnings.

Here's an example of a balance sheet:

Your Company's Name
Date: 1 March 2023
Balance Sheet

	2023 Current year
Assets	
Current assets:	
	-
Cash	
	$8,000.00
Accounts receivable	
	$3,000.00
Prepaid expenses	
	$1,000.00
Inventory	
	$3,000.00
Total current assets	
	$15,000.00
Property & equipment	
	$10,000.00
Charity	
	$0.00
Total Assets	
	$25,000.00
Liabilities	
Current liabilities:	
Accounts payable	
	$500.00
Accrued expenses	
	$0.00
Unearned revenue	
	$0.00
Total current liabilities	
	$500.00
Long-term debt	
	$3,000.00
Other long-term liabilities	
	$1,500.00
Total Liabilities	
	$5,000.00
Shareholder's Equity	
Investment capital	
	$10,000.00
Retained earnings	
	$10,000.00
Shareholder's Equity	
	$20,000.00
Total Liabilities & Shareholder's Equity	
	$25,000.00

Notice that the total assets amount is equal to the total liabilities plus equity amount: $25,000 (assets) = $5,000 (liabilities) + $20,000 (equity).

The balance sheet's primary use is determining your business's financial health. It'll be more apparent what we mean when we go over the financial analysis of a business.

Cash Flow Statement

This financial report measures the cash flow determined by three activities: operating activities, financing activities, and investment activities. Knowing the movement of cash for these activities allows you to fund operating expenses and investments and pay your business's debt. The cash flow statement also provides insight into the financial situation of your business. Like the income statement, the cash flow statement reports cash flow over a given period, such as a year. The three major components of the cash flow statement are as follows:

- **Operating activities:** These activities bring in or use cash in running the operations of your business. They capture all the cash in the income statement, except depreciation and amortization, because they're noncash expenses.
- **Investing activities:** The cash in this section refers to cash generated or used due to the purchase or sale of capital or short-term assets. It provides a quick insight into whether your

business has made gains or losses on its investments over time.

- **Financing activities:** These activities report the cash raised from sources such as investors, business owners, or banks, as well as cash used to pay debt or pay business owners in the form of dividends.

Here's an example of a cash flow statement:

Your Company's Name
Cash Flow Statement

For the year ending: 2023

Operating Activities	
Customers	
	$100,000.00
Other operations	
	$0.00
Cash paid for	
General operating and admin expenses	
	-$45,000.00
Wage expenses	
	-$12,000.00
Interest	
	$0.00
Income taxes	
	-$4,000.00
Net Profit From Operations	
$39,000.00	
Additions to cash	
Depreciation	
	$300.00
Amortization	
	$200.00
Subtractions from cash	
Net working capital	
	-$1,900.00
Total Cash From Operating Activities	
	$37,600.00
Investing Activities	
Cash receipts from	
Sale of equipment	
	$500.00
Bank loan	
	$1,000.00
Total Cash From Investing Activities	
	$1,500.00
Financing Activities	
Drawing/distribution	
	-$3,000.00
Repayment of loans	
	-$1,000.00
Total Cash From Financing Activities	
	-$4,000.00
Beginning cash	
$5,000.00	
Total change in cash	
$35,100.00	
Ending Cash	
	$40,100.00

Your business should have $40,100 in its bank account by the end of 2023, which you confirm with a bank statement.

Notice that the cash flow statement consists of components from the income statement and the balance sheet.

For this reason, you can look at the cash flow statement as the reconciler of the income statement and the balance sheet.

STEPS TO CREATE EFFECTIVE FINANCIAL REPORTS

If your business uses accounting software, you won't need to create financial statements manually; the accounting software will do this for you. Why, then, should you learn how to prepare financial reports? Well, you want to understand every financial statement so that you can use it properly for analysis and decision-making. Nearly all the businesses in the case study at the opening of this chapter prepared financial reports. However, almost none used them because they didn't understand them.

Learning to prepare financial statements provides you with the understanding you need for effective business financial performance analysis. That's why you need to ensure that all your numbers are accurate and have sources from which you derived them. Let's learn how to prepare the first financial report without further ado.

How to Prepare the Income Statement

Creating an income statement requires following the steps below:

- **Step 1—Decide your reporting period and date:** This period should reflect how you intend to use the income statement. It's worth creating an income statement each month for monthly budget reviews because figures like revenue go to your budget as actuals. Also, consider preparing income statements at each quarter's and financial year's end.
- **Step 2—Determine your total revenue:** Add all the income received for selling your products or services to obtain your total revenue over the chosen reporting period. If you sell products or services on credit, include the sales you made, whether you received payment or not.
- **Step 3—Figure out your total COGS:** Calculate the direct total costs incurred when producing and selling your products or services. Some of the expenses include raw materials, manufacturing, and delivery costs.
- **Step 4—Calculate your gross profit:** Subtract your total COGS from total revenue to get your gross profit.

- **Step 5—Calculate your total operating expenses:** These costs are indirect expenses incurred while running your business, such as insurance, rent, utilities, website hosting, and accounting software subscription.

- **Step 6—Work out your operating income:** Subtract your total operating costs from your gross profit to get your operating income like this: gross profit — operating expenses = operating income.

- **Step 7—Calculate the depreciation or amortization of your assets:** The simplest method for calculating the depreciation of each of your assets is to use an online MACRS depreciation calculator. However, we recommend speaking to a certified accountant on how to handle this, including amortization.

- **Step 8—Calculate profit or loss before interest and taxes:** Subtract depreciation and amortization from operating profit to determine profit or loss before interest and taxes like this: Profit or loss before interest and taxes = operating profit − depreciation and amortization.

- **Step 9—Work out interest and taxes:** The interest owed appears on your debt statements. Total all your interests and note the result in your accounting statement. Taxes to pay may include local, state, or federal taxes. Find an aggregate of your taxes and plug the number in your income statement.

- **Step 10—Calculate your net profit or loss:** Subtract interests and taxes calculated above to work out your net profit or loss, meaning that net profit = profit before interest and taxes – interest and taxes. If the result is a negative number, you've made a loss over your selected reporting period. Otherwise, you've made a profit.

Ensure you add your business's header to your income statement before sharing it with anyone. When you've finalized your income statement, you can transfer metrics such as your total revenue, expenses, and profit or loss to your budgeting tool as actuals for reviewing how you performed against the budget.

How to Create the Balance Sheet

Here are the steps to prepare your business's balance sheet:

- **Step 1—Determine the reporting date:** Choose a date to report your business's assets, liabilities, and equity. Typically, your reporting date would be at the end of the month, quarter, or financial year.

- **Step 2—Identify your assets and determine their total:** Identify each short-term asset and record its value. Calculate the total value of your short-term assets. Do the same with your long-term assets. Add the total of short-term and long-term assets to determine your total assets.
- **Step 3—Identify your liabilities and calculate their total:** Repeat Step 2 but on liabilities.
- **Step 4—Calculate your equity:** Since your business is privately held, your equity will be your retained earnings because you don't issue stock.
- **Step 5—Compare the sum of total liabilities and equity to total assets:** Calculate the sum of total liabilities and equity and compare it to total assets. Your balance sheet is correct if total liabilities plus equity equals total assets (assets = liabilities + equity). Otherwise, you'll need to revisit assets and liabilities to identify errors and correct them.

Your balance sheet is crucial for analyzing how indebted your business is. Sometimes, you may go deep in debt and need help to grow equity. If your equity isn't increasing yearly, you must understand why and address the culprit.

How to Make the Statement of Cash Flow

This financial report is crucial for cash flow analysis, cash management, and credit management. Understanding how to prepare it will also help you know where each of the numbers it reports comes from.

You can use direct or indirect methods to prepare the cash flow statement. The direct method requires adding income from your customers and subtracting all expenses. In contrast, the indirect method starts with the net income in the income statement of the same reporting period. It adjusts it for noncash inflows or outflows. This method is more straightforward and less time-consuming than the direct method, and we'll use it here.

With that said, here are the steps for preparing the cash flow statement (using the indirect method):

- **Step 1—Decide your reporting date and period:** The first step is to decide when to report your cash flow and what period to cover.
- **Step 2—Determine the opening balance:** This is the net income as reported in the income statement of the same reporting period.

- **Step 3—Add noncash expenses to your net income**: Identify and add noncash expenses from the income statement, such as depreciation and amortization. These expenses were deducted for accounting purposes but don't involve cash outflows.

- **Step 4—Determine your net working Capital**: Working capital is the difference between your current assets and liabilities captured on your balance sheet. Net working capital is the difference between a period's opening and closing working capital.

- **Step 5—Calculate your cash flow from operating activities**: Add your net working capital to the result of step 3 to obtain your cash flow from operating activities.

- **Step 6—Work out cash flow from investing activities**: Add cash generated for selling assets such as equipment or investments and subtract cash used to buy similar assets. The outcome is cash from investing activities.

- **Step 7—Work out cash flow from financing activities**: Add cash the business received from investors, loans, or the business owner and subtract cash used to pay back debt. The resulting figure is the net cash from financing activities.

- **Step 8—Calculate the closing balance:** Add the cash flows from operations, investing, and financing to determine the net cash during the reporting period (operations cash + investing cash + financing cash = net cash flow). The resulting figure tells you how much cash you've gained or lost during the period of interest.

For cash management, this is the statement to analyze. When your business loses cash, it's vital to understand where this is happening and close the leaks quickly. For example, suppose you're losing money from operations. In that case, it's time to delve deeper into your expenses, as reported in the income statement.

When you know how to prepare each of the three major financial statements, you'll use them with understanding. Even if you use financial reporting or accounting software such as Xero, Quickbooks, Sage, or Insight Software, you can spot issues with your financial statements. Most importantly, you can confidently use them for business decision-making, as will be discussed next.

INTERPRETING FINANCIAL REPORTS FOR BETTER DECISION-MAKING

Knowing how to prepare financial reports isn't enough; understanding how to analyze and interpret them for business decision-making is even more critical. This is where financial metrics come in handy, especially ratios used to gauge your company's financial health. Whoever interprets your business's financial statement will use financial metrics for decision-making.

In this next section, we'll focus on analyzing and interpreting the income statement, balance sheet, and cash flow statement.

How to Analyze the Income Statement

The analysis of the income statement comes down to three primary financial ratios. Raw numbers on the income statement are essential for calculating these ratios. All the critical financial ratios are related to profits. Here are these primary profit ratios:

Gross Profit Margin

As explained in the section on the income statement and its importance, gross profit margin tells you how much of the total revenue is available for net profit generation.

A gross profit margin of 60% means that for every $1 your business generates, $0.60 goes toward the bottom line. The question is, "What is a good gross profit margin?" The answer is that it depends on your industry and type of business. By doing industry research, you'll need to determine an acceptable gross profit margin. For example, a company that offers education and training in the US typically averages 53.4% in gross profit margin (FullRatio, n.d.).

If you take note of a lower gross profit margin, you can reduce COGS or increase the prices of—or sell more of —your products or services.

Operating Profit Margin

The operating profit margin takes the gross profit and subtracts operating expenses such as rent, insurance, utilities, website hosting, and software subscriptions.

You calculate the operating profit margin as follows:

Operating profit margin = operating profit/total revenue x 100.

For example, suppose your company makes $50,000 in operating profit during a specific reporting period from $120,000 in total revenue. In that case, your operating profit margin will be 41.7% ($50,000/$120,000 x 100 = 0.417 x 100 = 41.7%). For every dollar in revenue you make, $0.42 goes toward generating your bottom line.

No rule limits the size of your operating profit margin. The higher it is, the better your company is controlling overheads. You have more control over operating expenses, except taxes and interests. If you pay too much for insurance or software subscriptions, you can shop for cheaper ones. You can do the same for other overhead expenses, too.

You can also increase your operating profit margin in the same way you can ramp up your gross profit margin.

Net Profit Margin

This is the percentage of your revenue you generate after handling all your business expenses. You obtain it by dividing your net income by your total revenue and expressing the results in a percentage as follows:

Net profit margin = net profit/total revenue x 100

If your business makes $35,000 in net profit from $120,000 in total revenue, your net profit margin will be 29.2% ($35,000/$120,000 x 100 = 0.292 x 100 = 29.2%). This figure is neither good nor bad because this depends on your budget and industry average.

The same methods of increasing your gross and operating profit margins also shoot up your net profit margin.

When you analyze your profit margins over a period of time, you can determine if your business's financial performance is improving or declining. It's also easier to identify initiatives responsible for the patterns you observe.

How to Analyze the Balance Sheet

Balance sheet analysis and interpretation allow you to determine your company's financial position. It answers whether your company can pay its debt and still survive. You use three financial ratios to perform a basic balance sheet analysis and interpretation.

Current Ratio

The current ratio determines if you have enough current assets to convert to cash to pay your short-term liabilities—a measure of liquidity. Calculate it as follows:

Current ratio = current assets/current liabilities

The higher the current ratio, the easier it will be to pay your short-term obligations - meaning you won't have to sell your capital assets to pay your short-term debt. Even if you wanted to, your creditors might be impatient as they wait for you because it generally takes longer to sell long-term assets.

Suppose your business has $50,000 in current assets and $26,000 in short-term liabilities. In that case, its current ratio will be 1.92:1 ($50,000/$26,000:$26,000/$26,000 = 1.92:1). This is good because your business has more than enough current assets to turn into cash and settle your short-term debt.

Keeping this ratio higher than 1:1 is crucial, or you'll be in a tight spot.

Quick Ratio

The quick ratio, also termed the acid test ratio, performs a similar function as the current ratio. It focuses only on highly liquid current assets such as cash to settle short-term debt.

You calculate it as follows:

Quick ratio = (cash and cash equivalents + accounts receivable + marketable securities)/short-term liabilities

Accounts receivable is nothing more than money your customers owe you for products or services.

Suppose your business has cash and cash equivalents and accounts receivable of $40,000. Your acid test ratio is 1.54:1 ($ 40,000/ $ 26,000: $ 26,000/ $ 26,000 = 1.54:1), which is more than enough.

Debt-to-Equity Ratio

The debt-to-equity (DE) ratio measures how much your business relies on debt compared to investment money. This ratio is crucial for debt management. You calculate the DE ratio like this:

DE ratio = total debt/equity

The less your business depends on debt, the more profit it'll make for a given revenue. Your equity will also increase as more profit stays in the business.

Next, suppose that your business's debt is $30,000 and equity is $50,000. Your DE ratio will be 0.6:1, meaning that for every dollar of equity, you owe $0.60. This result means you can predominantly operate your business using your own money.

A good DE ratio varies from industry to industry and the type of business. Don't fret if yours is 1:1 or 2:1 because that's generally considered good (Freshbooks, 2021).

How to Interpret and Analyze the Cash Flow Statement

Your best bet regarding cash management is analyzing and interpreting your cash flow statement.

Knowing how much of your income was cash generated during a specific period is crucial. Also, you must find out if you have enough available money to pay your current debt. Your cash flow statement's financial ratios help you figure out all we've just gone over.

Cash Flow Coverage Ratio

This ratio helps you determine how well your business generates profit in cash to pay off all its debt. Like the balance sheet's financial ratios, the cash flow coverage ratio depicts how financially healthy your business is. This ratio is typically calculated over the course of a year instead of monthly.

You can calculate your cash flow coverage ratio by using this formula:

Cash flow coverage ratio = net cash flow from operating activities/total debt

We will use an example to demonstrate how to use the above formula. Suppose your business has a total debt of $23,000; during a particular year, it makes $20,000 in operating profit. Its cash flow coverage ratio will be

0.87:1 ($20,000/$23,000:$20,000/$20,0000 = 0.87:1). A cash flow coverage ratio less than 1:1 is concerning because it means you don't have enough cash on hand to pay off all your debt.

The more net cash from operations you generate for a higher than 1:1 cash flow coverage ratio, the better your business's financial health. This higher ratio is worth striving to achieve.

Current Liability Coverage Ratio

This ratio measures how much cash you have to pay your current liabilities in a given period. The formula for calculating the current liability coverage ratio is as follows:

Current liability ratio = net cash from operating activities/current liabilities

This calculation will always be accurate for the annual current liability coverage ratio. However, your current liability can change from month to month, leading to an inaccurate measure of monthly current liability coverage ratios. It's a good idea to use the average current liability to improve the accuracy of your analysis. Let's illustrate this.

Suppose that you want to calculate the current liability coverage ratio for the month of June. The opening and closing current liabilities were $9,000 and $10,600 respectively. Your average current liability was $9,800 (($9,000+$10,600)/2 = $19,600/2 = $9,800). If your net cash from operating activities was $20,000, your current liability coverage ratio was 2.04:1 ($20,000/$9,800:$9,800/$9,800 = 2.04:1). Your company has money to fund its short-term debt.

The higher this ratio is, the better it is for your business. Otherwise, you might need help to pay your current liabilities, such as loan interest.

Cash Flow Margin Ratio

This financial ratio tells you how much new cash you generate during a given operating period. Instead of focusing only on net profit, you also figure out how much cash you make for every dollar of revenue you generate.

You can determine the cash flow margin ratio by using this formula:

Cash flow margin ratio = net cash from operating activities/total revenue

Now, let's go over how to calculate this ratio from your cash flow and income statements. Suppose your business generates $100,000 in revenue and $37,000 in net cash flow from operations. Your cash flow margin ratio will be 0.37:1 ($37,000/$100,000:$37,000/$37,000 = 0.37:1). For every dollar of revenue you made, you generated $0.37 in cash.

Whether you run a cash-based business or you also sell on credit, you want this ratio to be as high as possible.

It's time to apply what you've learned above to your business. Create all three financial statements of your business at the end of the current month. Once done, you can go about the following:

- **Income statement:** Calculate your gross profit margin, operating profit margin, and net profit margin. For each of them, determine if it's good or bad. If it's terrible, determine why and create an action plan to address your identified issues. Even if a given profit margin is good, are there ways you can make it better? Create an improvement plan and immediately execute it. Your action plan will likely revolve around maximizing revenues and minimizing costs to improve profit margins. Make your action plan as specific as possible. For example, increase prices by 10%.
- **Balance sheet:** Calculate your current, quick, and DE ratios. Evaluate whether each is where you want it or not. Whether a ratio is good or

not, figure out how to improve it. Essentially, your focus here will be on increasing your assets (short- and long-term) and minimizing your liabilities.

- **Cash flow statement:** Determine your cash flow coverage, current liability coverage, and cash flow margin ratios. Does your business have the cash to cover its short-term debt and to fund operations? If not, work out how to bring in more money, such as running a campaign to get as many invoices paid as possible. This strategy could also include creating an email sequence to request your customers to pay you. You may even consider selling your securities, such as stocks or bonds.

For the above analysis to be more effective, consider setting benchmarks and goals for the actual financial metrics and ratios. Tracking these metrics and ratios over multiple reporting periods will reveal business problems that block you from achieving your goals and benchmarks. As you address those issues, you'll better manage your business's financial health, including better cash flow and debt management.

Successful business owners face facts irrespective of where they might lead. As you read and analyze your financial statements, you'll face realities you may not like. It may be difficult, but you must meet and address them without being emotional. Business is an intellectual game that needs to be played more from your intellect than your emotions.

Your understanding of financial reporting can indicate how well your marketing is working. It'll enable you to allocate marketing resources in a way that improves your financial performance. Speaking of which, it's time to turn our attention to how to use marketing to improve your bottom line in the next chapter.

3

BOOSTING PROFITS THROUGH EFFECTIVE MARKETING

L et's start this chapter with a question: How do you differentiate your business in a saturated market such as the fitness industry? Two companies can sell fitness clothing, but one may fail while the other thrives. It's all about positioning your brand—an essential marketing function. A case in point is how Ben Francis, CEO and co-founder of Gymshark, built his business from the start. Francis created physique-enhancing fitness clothing he'd be happy to wear using sewing skills he learned from his grandmother.

Gymshark's masterstroke marketing genius was implementing influencer marketing in the weightlifting game. Influencer marketing takes advantage of the popularity of individuals with a large following to sell products or services. Gymshark sent its products to weightlifting influencers who liked what they saw. Through videos and other media, these influencers shared information about Gymshark and its clothing with their communities. This fundamental marketing approach has turned Gymshark into a billion-dollar company (Vallone, 2021).

Gymshark's story indicates how transformative proper marketing can be for your business. Francis hit on the right marketing approach almost by chance—but you don't have to. We will share with you in this chapter what types of marketing can work for businesses in all kinds of industries. Before we do that, though, let's talk about why you need marketing in the first place.

THE IMPORTANCE OF MARKETING

Gymshark is an excellent example of the impact of marketing on small businesses. When you get marketing wrong, you can pay the ultimate price—failure. Even with thousands in capital, your business can fail due to the wrong marketing. To illustrate this, let's consider the story of the late Lumos, a technology company that created machine learning-based internet-connected devices.

Lumos was founded in 2014 by first-time entrepreneurs Pritesh Sankhe, Tarkeshwar Singh, and Yash Kotak. Only a year later, Lumos collapsed. A postmortem on the company revealed various factors contributing to its failure, including creating a cost-ineffective product. The big issue was that Lumos didn't know its ideal customer. Therefore, it tried to sell its product to anyone who cared to listen (Failory, n.d.). This approach is a trap that inexperienced entrepreneurs often fall into.

Marketing is everything your business does to attract and retain customers. Marketing techniques include product or service design, advertising, customer service, and customer research. When done correctly, marketing leads to the sales of your products or services. Because of marketing's far-reaching influence on your business, it's necessary to understand in what ways it benefits you.

- **It helps identify the right type of customer.**
  When you've identified your ideal customer, you'll know where to find them. Proper identification makes it cheaper to find and convert them into customers.
- **It builds the trust you need to make sales.**
  People buy from brands they trust. For instance, you could offer your potential

customers value through case studies, ebooks, or videos. This non-selling approach fosters a relationship that builds trust and simplifies converting your potential customers into buyers.

- **It spreads the word about your business.** You can have the best product or service in the world, but you won't make many sales unless your target audience knows about it.
- **It opens up money-making opportunities.** As more and more people interact with your business, you get to understand them better. These opportunities allow you to identify future products or services to offer them.
- **It makes you more competitive.** Without effective marketing, your competitors will outperform you. This competitive drive forces big companies like Apple and Amazon to keep marketing themselves, their products, and their services.

The benefits alluded to above indicate that marketing makes revenue generation possible. It doesn't matter whether your business is a newbie or an oldie; it needs proper marketing. This point brings us to specific marketing strategies, especially for small businesses like yours.

CRAFTING A WINNING MARKETING STRATEGY ON A BUDGET

Proper marketing of your business begins with having a budget-friendly and winning marketing strategy. This strategy gives the overarching game plan for materializing your business's goals. Unlike the marketing plan, it doesn't focus on the tactics you'll use to nail your business's goals. A marketing strategy answers who your business's ideal buyer is, how you'll reach them, who your competitors are, and the solution you offer to your target buyer.

Seven Steps to Create Your Marketing Strategy

Here are seven steps for creating your marketing strategy:

Step 1: Define Your Business and Marketing Goals

This first step should align with the budget you created in Chapter 1. It's also the most crucial step to complete because it sets the foundation for the rest of your marketing strategy. The primary business goal your marketing should help achieve is the operating revenue. Regarding your marketing strategy, two critical goals you should consider to realize your revenue are the number of sales leads and customers to generate.

Every business goal you set should be Specific, Measurable, Achievable, Relevant, and Time-bound. This approach makes up the helpful acronym "SMART." An example of a company goal could be "To generate 5,000 sales leads by the end of the year."

Step 2: Research Your Target Market and Create Your Buyer Persona

The second step is understanding who you will sell your products or services to. Business owners often complete most of this research before producing their products or services. Otherwise, you could create a product or service your target audience doesn't want and make the same mistake as Lumos.

The starting point of researching your target audience is understanding their demographics—characteristics such as age, gender, occupation, income level, college education, and marital status. More importantly, you must understand your target customers' pains and desires. These are emotional reasons that drive your target customers' buying decisions.

When you understand your target customer, it's time to craft your buyer persona. This fictional character describes your perfect buyer. When defining your buyer persona, include their daily routines, pains and challenges, and how their life would look when they've addressed their main issues. A paragraph is large enough to describe your buyer persona.

Step 3: Research Your Competitors and Industry

Your target audience is likely already buying products or services from your competitors. It's vital to determine why they're buying from your competitors. This information gives you ideas on how to differentiate your business.

Your research begins with entering industry keywords in search engines and visiting a couple of your competitors' websites and social media pages. Some features to look for include what products or services your competitors sell, pricing, and how and where they promote what they offer.

During this research, check what's trending in your industry. Pay attention to what customers in your industry are saying. Chances are that they're unsatisfied with some products, services, or the customer service they receive. This research gives you a gap you can take advantage of.

Step 4: Define Your Brand's Message

After researching your target audience, the industry, and competitors, you'll identify how to position your business. Positioning differentiates your business from your competitors in the eyes of your target audience. You position your business by defining its brand's message.

The value proposition is central to your business's message—what you offer your target audience and what you stand for. Think carefully about what value you add to your target audience. When you have your value proposition, you can blend it with your business's aesthetics, such as its logo, brand tone and voice, colors, fonts, and imagery. Also, carefully choose your words and phrases to deliver your central message. Ultimately, your brand should define who you are and what you offer your target audience.

Step 5: Determine Marketing Channels to Use

The next step is to decide what marketing channels you will use to connect with your target audience. Marketing channels are media through which you communicate your brand's message and connect with your target audience. When you researched your competitors and the industry, you may have realized what channels you'll begin with.

The typical marketing channels across industries include social media, blogs, and email. This isn't to say that media like newspapers, magazines, and direct mail are out of the question. You usually need to test and prove each media before you adopt it. Initially, it helps to go with the channels others in your industry use. We'll talk more about marketing channels shortly.

Step 6: Determine Your Marketing Budget

The size of your marketing budget depends on what business and marketing goals you want to achieve. It costs money to generate sales leads and convert them into customers. The marketing cost of acquiring a buyer is called a customer acquisition cost (CAC). You can get this number from your industry data if you don't already have it. Let's go over exactly how you can arrive at your marketing budget.

Suppose you want to acquire 5,000 customers in a particular year to generate annual revenue. If your CAC is $10, you'll need to spend 5,000 times $10 = $50,000 for your marketing. Add your marketing operational costs to this figure to determine your total marketing budget. If your annual marketing operational budget is $12,000, your comprehensive marketing will be $62,000.

Step 7: Determine Your Key Performance Indicators

The next step is to measure your progress as you implement your marketing strategy. You measure your marketing performance by using key performance indicators (KPIs). The KPIs you measure depend on the marketing and business goals you'd like to achieve.

For a goal to acquire 5,000 customers, one of the KPIs to consider is the number of sales leads you generate per month. Another crucial one is the monthly number of sales leads you convert into customers. Ensure you also measure your CAC to ensure you don't overspend on your marketing.

If unsure what KPIs to track, check your industry's marketing data for ideas.

Low-Cost Marketing Channels to Consider Using

You don't need a huge marketing budget to find and convert your target audience into raving customers; it takes identifying the right message and channels and connecting with your target audience. At this point, you have the right message, and you now need the proper marketing channels. Here are some low-cost marketing channels to consider:

- **Social media:** The top way consumers discover products on social media is through advertising followed by unpaid-for posts. This approach is an excellent opportunity to tap into the nearly 5 billion social media users (Sprout Social, 2023). We recommend spreading your presence across three or so social media channels because you can find consumers across multiple platforms.

- **Email:** Over half of all email users check it first thing in the morning. With email, every $1 spent generates $36, a return on investment (ROI) of 3,600% (Holovach, 2023). The good news is that you can start using numerous email marketing software for free up to a certain level. This technique allows you to use email marketing software and generate revenue before paying for it. You can also use email to generate leads and convert them into customers.

- **Blog:** While millions of blogs exist, the desire for written content hasn't stopped yet. People continue to actively read blogs, which is why they're a popular marketing channel. A blog provides more than enough space to provide valuable content, from a few hundred words to thousands of words. Using a blog, you can attract your target audience to your website and turn them into sales leads for free. The key is creating content that readers and search engines such as Google and Bing like.

- **Collaborating with influencers:** This option involves collaborating with a person with a large following that matches your target audience. You can mostly find influencers on social media platforms. When an influencer shares or reviews your product or service, their followers payattention—and some may even buy. If your target audience includes millennials, you'll be thrilled to know that 50% of them trust influencer product recommendations (Rodrigue, 2023).

Whichever channel you use, aim to share content your target audience wants. The reason is that content readers want information that helps them solve their issues. That's why some content you create should include guides, how-to information, and behind-the-scenes content on how you produce your product or services. When you research them and your competitors, you can determine what type of content your target audience wants. You'll also discover in what format—video, audio, or text—you should focus the bulk of your content creation on. Sharing the right content in the correct format can contribute toward improved ROI.

MEASURING AND ENHANCING YOUR MARKETING ROI

There's only one way to determine the effectiveness of your marketing, and that's measuring its ROI. For your marketing to be profitable, it should cost less than you spend. You can also use marketing ROI to determine the success of any marketing initiative, such as advertising campaigns, which are, put plainly, a series of actions you take to advertise your products or services. More importantly, you can use marketing ROI to compare the performance of one channel against another. To use marketing ROI, you first need to know how to calculate it.

How to Measure Your Marketing ROI

There's one way to measure marketing ROI irrespective of your marketing type. Here's the formula: marketing ROI = marketing profit/marketing cost x 100, where marketing profit = number of customers generated x average sales price – marketing operational costs – marketing cost.

It's easy to measure your marketing cost, whether at a campaign or individual marketing initiative level. Working out the profit from your marketing can be tricky unless you track the source of each of your customers and know your marketing operational costs.

The growth of digital marketing has brought forth tools that can help track the sources of your customers. If you're doing content marketing, you can rely on tools such as Google Analytics since social media analytics comes in handy when you run social media ads.

Marketing operational costs cover expenses for creating promotional material such as ads, blogs, and videos. You must also include the cost of supplies and software used in your marketing.

Let's go over how to calculate marketing ROI from an ad. Suppose your business spends $2,000 running social media ads during a specific month. It costs you $300 to hire someone to create and monitor those ads. Your ads receive ten clicks, of which seven result in orders. The average sales price you realize per customer is thus $2,500.

Your marketing ROI = marketing profit/marketing cost x 100 = (number of customers generated x average sales price – marketing operational costs – marketing cost)/marketing cost x 100 = (7 x $2,500 – $300 – $2,000)/$2,000 x 100 = $15,200/$2,000 x 100 = 760%.

The key to calculating your marketing ROI is having the necessary metrics. Ensure you know your marketing costs and how many customers your marketing efforts generate.

A good marketing ROI depends on various factors, including your type of business and the industry in which it operates. Having said that, if you get a 500% marketing ROI, you'll be doing well in many companies. Though rare, bringing it to 1,000% indicates an exceptional marketing performance (Leone, 2019).

Enhancing Your Marketing ROI

If you calculate your marketing ROI and aren't happy with it, how can you improve it? Well, there are numerous strategies you can use for this purpose, including the following:

- **Trying different offers:** The offer can make or break your marketing. Your primary approach to making offers should be to create irresistible offers. An offer includes the price of your product or service, the guarantee, the payment options, and the bonuses. For example, you can offer a 50% discount, a 2-year warranty, and bonuses whose value exceeds the price of your product. Even with reasonable offers, try different ones to determine the one with the highest marketing ROI.
- **Testing different marketing channels:** Your ideal customers can be on social media platforms, search engines, blogs, and news

websites. Test these marketing channels to determine which gives the best ROI.

- **Experimenting with different content formats:** People prefer specific content formats. For instance, some prefer video because they're visual learners, while others enjoy reading. To optimize the number of customers, consider creating content in various formats and experimenting to see which works best. In some cases, such as with ads, you can use video and text simultaneously.

The above ideas provide the starting point for enhancing your marketing ROI. Consider other ideas you can try, including improved understanding of your target market and enhancing your content or ads. When you find a combination of ideas that brings about the best marketing ROI, use it for as long as it's working.

Implementing the proper marketing to woo your target audience can usher your business into the league of best performers. A case in point is Coffee & Contracts, a company that provides marketing tools to real estate professionals. This company was founded by Haley Ingram, a real estate professional who has grown it to $1.86 million in revenue annually (Taylor, n.d.). How does Coffee & Contracts get customers?

Well, Ingram didn't start off creating a company like this. She posted on Instagram to try and find customers she could sell homes to and for as a real estate agent. To her astonishment, she got customers *and* attracted the attention of other real estate professionals who wanted help with social media marketing. It wasn't until after her friend introduced her to the membership concept that Ingram surpassed the limitations of geography and began serving many more real estate professionals. Since then, her business has grown by leaps and bounds.

Consider your business and decide what marketing channel and content format suits it best. Video content works for many industries and businesses and could be a good starting point. Most importantly, craft an irresistible offer that will keep your potential customers up at night if they don't take it. Include a deadline in your offer, as well, to ensure they snatch up the offer immediately.

If you do the above, you'll be on the right path to growing your business. Be careful about growing your business too fast, as you might risk failing to provide high-quality customer service. The point is that you need to manage business growth effectively. On that note, the upcoming chapter will provide insights into managing your time and resources effectively to sustain growth while maintaining quality business operations.

Dear Reader,

We hope you're finding "The Essential Small Business Guide to Financial Management" enlightening and insightful on your entrepreneurial journey. Your opinion matters immensely to us, and we kindly request a few moments of your time to leave a review on Amazon.

Your review serves as a valuable compass for fellow entrepreneurs, helping them navigate the path to financial success with confidence. It also provides us with essential feedback to improve and tailor our content to your needs.

To leave a review on Amazon:

1. Grab Your Device: Open the Amazon app or visit Amazon.com on your computer or mobile device.

2. Log in: Sign in to your Amazon account. If you don't have one, you can quickly create an account.

3. Scan the QR Code: Use your device's camera to scan the QR Code below. This will take you directly to the book's review page on Amazon.

4. Write Your Review: Share your thoughts, insights, and feedback about the book. We appreciate both positive reviews and constructive criticism—it all helps us grow and serve you better.

5. Submit Your Review: Click 'Submit' to publish your review and make it accessible to others.

Your contribution to our community of entrepreneurs is immeasurable, and we thank you in advance for taking the time to leave your review.

Happy Reading and Reviewing!

With warm regards,
Dr. Bryan Raya
DBR Publishing
Doing Business Right

4

BALANCING EFFICIENCY AND GROWTH

Have you ever wished there were more than 24 hours in a day? We know how it feels when the day ends before you can review your business's budget, call an important customer, or create a content marketing plan. Business owners leave some of our critical work undone no matter how hard we work. This approach negatively impacts our revenue generation and limits our profits. So, how do we escape this paralyzing situation and get all our tasks done? The answer is to employ proper time management skills—and not only to accomplish all our tasks but also to do them efficiently and to improve the financial performance of your business. This chapter will delve into precisely how to do this, but let's first look at what time management is and how beneficial it is.

TIME MANAGEMENT FOR SMALL BUSINESSES

Just think about what you could accomplish if you used your time effectively! You'd be astonished at how much you could get done within a short amount of time. As entrepreneurs, we tend to be effective at idea generation but not so much with business operations. Successfully operating a business demands proper coordination of your tasks—and when you have time management skills, this is what you'll achieve.

Having good time management skills doesn't suggest you can manage time, as, let's face it, time cannot be controlled by anyone. Yes, working on something is about owning it, which you can't do with time. Time is either always going to be fixed or limited. Your job, then, is to work within the available time.

The basis of time management is planning, organizing, and scheduling tasks to accomplish your business goals. It's doing this that allows you to perform not just any task but activities you know will have the most positive impact on your business. When you have improved your time management skills, your business will improve all its activities—operations, financial management, and marketing. For instance, you'll schedule time to budget and review your costs periodically. This process will help you identify areas where you're leaking money and patch them up, leading to increased profits. There are many more ways you and your business can benefit, as will be discussed next.

The Importance of Time Management for Business Owners

Successful and unsuccessful business owners each have 24 hours per day to work with. Why does one business owner win while another struggles? One significant contributing factor is how successful and unsuccessful business owners use their time. Unsuccessful business owners juggle numerous tasks and achieve little. They mistakenly confuse hard work with effectiveness— doing the right things at the right time. If you'd like to be a successful business owner, and we assume you would, then you must learn how to use your time. Here are more reasons for this:

- **It reduces stress.** Managing your time well means focusing on tasks that matter the most and can improve your business. Feeling in control reduces stress, which improves your health—a crucial element of performing well in any task.

- **It improves your efficiency and effectiveness.**
Time management skills minimize distractions,
leading to more effective use of your daily 24
hours and energy.
- **You'll have more free time.** Your improved
time management skills enable you to finish
tasks on time.
- **It enhances your decision-making.** Good time
management skills calm you down and enable
you to think clearly. This allows you to evaluate
the business challenges you face rationally.
- **It helps you regain your confidence.** When
you tick off essential tasks in your schedule and
meet deadlines, your confidence will shoot up.
When you've skyrocketed your confidence,
you'll have the guts to take on tasks that grow
your business in a big way.

Review how you currently use your time each day. If
you aren't sure how you're using it, try this out in the
next two weeks: Record each business activity you do
each hour of each day. Analyze how much time you
spend on each of your business's functions. From there,
determine what impact those activities have had on
your business. When done, ask yourself how the
improved use of your time can benefit you and your

business. As you do this, consider the efficiency paradox discussed in the next section.

THE PARADOX OF EFFICIENCY AND GROWTH

Does business productivity or efficiency lead to business growth? Before you answer that question, imagine this situation: You arrive early one morning at your work desk, fire up your computer, and shoot out ten emails. Sounds okay so far. In no time, though, you're caught up in receiving responses to those emails and sending even more emails. Before you realize it, you've already spent more than an unplanned hour on emails and are still in the loop of sending and receiving emails. Will your productivity in handling these emails result in business growth? Well, not necessarily.

Efficiency isn't synonymous with effectiveness. You might be trapped in sending and responding to emails unrelated to your business goals. You may have realized that no matter how productive you are at responding to emails, you keep receiving more. If you stay on this task, your business won't benefit much when you finish up for the day. This focus on increasing efficiency at the expense of factors such as quality is called the efficiency paradox.

You'll feel like you're making progress when stuck in the efficiency paradox. Unbeknownst to you, you're producing low-quality work because your focus is elsewhere. Instead of growing your business, your efficiency may lead to the opposite. For instance, customer complaints may increase—as will online negative reviews. In turn, you'll struggle to get new customers, and current ones may start doing business with your competitors.

Now, we're not saying chasing after productivity is wrong. You should align your productivity with your business goals. We don't want your business to be like someone driving a car at 100 mph—but going in the wrong direction. You want to strive for the ultimate goal of high productivity *and* moving in the right direction.

There are two other drawbacks of being trapped in the efficiency paradox.

- **You miss business growth opportunities.**
  When focused on improving efficiency, you pay little attention to ideas that can revolutionize your business. A case in point occurred at Xerox, the famous maker and seller of office equipment, in the late 1960s. An engineer shared with his boss a technology he believed

would surpass their existing one. His boss dismissed him because his attention was entirely devoted to improving the efficiency of existing equipment. Fortunately, Xerox's research division heard the idea and implemented it. In a decade, the new printing technology overtook their traditional printing technology. You can imagine what might have happened to Xerox had no one acted on that idea! While chasing after efficiency, recognize that it's only one-half of your business success. The other is business growth.

- **Your excessive focus on efficiency can cause burnout.** When you excessively drive efficiency, you're putting pressure on yourself. This pressure can negatively impact your performance because it may create stress. Not only does stress prevent clear thinking, but it can also decrease productivity.

The efficiency paradox isn't good for your business. However, this doesn't mean you need to eliminate business efficiency. It would be best if you were efficient while growing your business simultaneously. The key is to find ways to balance business efficiency with business growth. The following section will provide some methods of doing just this.

How to Achieve Both Efficiency and Business Growth

Business efficiency and growth aren't mutually exclusive; they're both necessary in the success equation of a business. How do you balance the two and avoid the efficiency paradox? Here are four broad concepts that will help you:

- **Find ways to manage your time effectively.**
  Make time management a high priority in all of your activities.
- **Test new ideas as quickly as possible.**
  Constant evolution ensures consistent growth, especially in our modern era of rapid changes in customers and technology.
- **Schedule thinking time.** Take at least an hour a week and think about your business—where it is, where it's going, and how you plan to get there. Only entertain thoughts and ideas about your business, its goals, and how it will achieve them.
- **Review what you've accomplished regularly.**
  Be sure your daily and weekly tasks align with your *current* business goals.

Is your business getting caught up in the efficiency paradox? If so, implement better time management strategies, test new ideas quickly, schedule thinking time, reflect on your business, and regularly review your accomplishments to balance business efficiency and growth. Regarding time management, knowing how you use your time is crucial. This approach demands that you deliberately apply the following time management strategies.

TIME MANAGEMENT STRATEGIES

As we said earlier, one of the solutions to defeating the efficiency paradox is effective time management. Not only will being an effective time manager maximize your profits, but it'll also protect your health. You become an effective time manager by using strategies such as the following:

- **Automating your business:** Every business conducts routine and nonroutine tasks. It's easier to systemize and automate routine tasks because they're repeatable. Some of your business's processes that you can automate include email marketing using email automation software, customer service through chatbots, and content creation using artificial intelligence (AI) tools. Doing this frees up more time, which you can use to focus on nonroutine tasks such as testing new ideas for business growth.

- **Delegating.** As business owners, we're used to wearing many hats and doing multiple business tasks, especially in the beginning. It's not unusual to simultaneously be the chief executive officer, technology officer, marketer, salesperson, bookkeeper, and product creator. We likely don't have to tell you that doing so many business tasks is a recipe for burnout and failure, but a reminder never hurts. One of the solutions to this is to delegate or outsource tasks that you're not good at. For example, if content creation isn't one of your strengths, hand it over to a more competent professional.

- **Prioritizing your tasks.** The tasks you execute each day don't all carry the same weight regarding their impact on your business. Some move you quickly toward your goals, while others sustain current business performance. Because you have a fixed amount of time and can't complete all those tasks, you must prioritize certain ones to achieve your business goals. Once you've prioritized your tasks, do the first one until it's complete before moving to the next. This technique is crucial because it's only after you've accomplished a task that you'll see its impact on your business's performance. Continue from one responsibility to the next until all of them are complete.

- **Scheduling your tasks.** Lack of organization is one of the enemies of effective time management. While prioritization adds structure to your tasks, it's even better if you can schedule them. Scheduling allows you to handle expected and unforeseen events and control your time daily. Scheduling also helps you care for your health by including breaks to take your mind off taxing work.
- **Scheduling time to review your day.** Reflect on how well you performed your business activities. Recording or journaling your thoughts for future reference is a good idea. You can also use this time to reflect on the progress of your business toward its goals.

Which of the previous time management strategies are you currently using? How are they working for you so far? Having time management strategies is great, but you need to review their impact on your business. If a particular technique doesn't work, it's worth trying another. However, many of these techniques work if you implement them with discipline. Initially, it'll be difficult because they won't be your habitual way of doing things. Give them sufficient time, though, and they will become habits. Once that happens, you'll be astonished by how much more effective you become.

We wouldn't have done our duty in this section if we didn't talk about time wasters we all encounter daily. Effectively managing time wasters is one of the most crucial time management skills.

Avoid Time Wasters

Time wasters are activities that consume time, reduce productivity, and prevent you from growing your business. You can think of them as distractors that impede concentration and sway you from achieving your goals. Knowing the different kinds of time wasters and how to manage them is vital. Our focus here will be on these time wasters:

- **Social media:** When you consider that an average social media user has eight accounts, you can spend more than an hour a day on this time waster (Ruby, 2023). You can avoid wasting time on social media by selecting a block of 20-30 minutes to check your social media feeds.
- **Multitasking:** This practice may appear to save you time, but it doesn't. When you do serious

business work, it leads to poor-quality work that may require revisions.

- **Email:** Frequently checking your emails disrupts your attention to your work and foils your productivity. A good practice is to allocate time for handling email, say about 30 minutes in the morning and another 30 in the afternoon.
- **Push notifications:** These interrupt you and shift your focus to unscheduled tasks—plain and simple. Block all notifications you've created and avoid allowing new ones.
- **Procrastination:** This can be avoided by prioritizing and scheduling your tasks.
- **Avoiding the delegation of tasks:** This forces you to spend your precious time on tasks you're not particularly strong in.

This chapter hammered the importance of managing your time to maximize your business's performance. It's crucial to perform tasks that are important to maximizing your profits and lengthening the life of your business. If you realize that you sometimes devote your time to unnecessary tasks, don't be hard on yourself, as new habits can take a while to develop. Whatever you do, though, don't fall into the trap of the efficiency paradox. Your time management skills will help increase the financial performance of your business.

Review how you currently use your time and identify opportunities to incorporate what you've learned here. Unless you do this, it'll be hard to expand your business due to the challenging nature of the task. It also takes careful financial planning to execute your business expansion plan. Don't worry if you haven't thought about expanding your business yet because we will tackle this subject in the next chapter.

5

FINANCIAL PLANNING FOR EXPANSION

Do you feel your business is ready for expansion? If so, you need to understand what you're putting your business into, what challenges you'll face, and how to handle them successfully. You also need a financial plan to ensure you have sufficient resources for the expansion. Before looking at the development of your business and how to create the financial plan you need, let's go over what's involved in financial planning.

WHAT IS FINANCIAL PLANNING?

Financial planning is evaluating your business's financial situation and allocating the finances to fund the required business growth. Don't mistake a budget for a financial plan. Yes, a budget is part of a business's economic plan, but it focuses on allocating financial resources for operations. A financial plan covers more ground, including financial projections of revenue and cash flow, capital expenditures, and risks that may hinder the achievement of your business growth.

The primary purpose of a financial plan is to help you set achievable short- and long-term business goals, mitigate risks, and make informed decisions. Here are the five major components of a detailed financial plan:

- **Conduct a revenue forecast:** This is what business budgeting helps you create. The forecast should cover the short- and long-term to show what the business intends to achieve.
- **Forecast your business's expenses:** This should include COGS and operating costs. Figure out the forecast gross profit, operating profit, and net profit. It's crucial to use accurate expenses for your forecast to be closer to reality. By the end of forecasting your revenue and expenses, you'll have the projected income statement.
- **Determine the break-even point:** The point where your revenue equals expenses is called the break-even point. To make a profit, your revenue should exceed the figure at the break-

even point. Using accurate financial data to determine the break-even point for sound decision-making is crucial.

- **Determine the cash flow projection:** Cash is to your business what blood is to your body. You don't want to run out because that would spell trouble. A cash flow projection will help you identify periods when you'll have insufficient cash flows. You can proactively plan how to find cash to cover expenses during those periods.
- **Create the forecast balance sheet:** This forecast estimates the net worth of your business. To generate this forecast, you must compile a list of your assets and liabilities.

Your work doesn't stop with having a financial plan. You need to take the crucial step of putting the plan into action. It might be necessary to adjust it when your business generates actual numbers. Crucially, you must compare your actual financial figures with your projections to ensure you achieve your business goals. You will need a financial plan even when you want to expand your business.

CREATING A GROWTH-ORIENTED FINANCIAL PLAN

All right, let's say you've stabilized your business financially, and you want to expand it to another level. Reasons for expanding your business vary from company to company. They may include penetrating a new market, adding more products, or buying another venture. Whatever your reason for expansion is, you need an accurate growth-focused financial plan.

Your financial plan for business expansion should answer four essential questions:

- How will the business generate cash as it expands?
- What financial resources does your business need to reach its expansion goals?
- What is your operating budget when you take into account the expansion?
- How will your business handle finance risks as it expands?

With these questions in your mind, you can begin to create your growth-focused financial plan. Here are the steps to follow:

- **Create your business expansion strategy.** The first thing to figure out is why you want to expand your business and the goals you want to nail. With your goals set, think about how you'll achieve them and what resources you'll need. It's also crucial to ask yourself if your business has the cash flow to support your growth ambitions. You may not know how much you'll need until you finish the next step, but this brainstorming is necessary before committing too much time to your growth goals.
- **Create a forecast of your business finances.** Your financial projections depend on the kind of expansion you want to accomplish. Suppose it's about entering new markets with the same products or services. In that case, your financial data can help establish your projections. Otherwise, you'll need to research the industry you're expanding into for the financial data required. Make sure that all your assumptions are backed by thorough research, as this will ensure your financial projections are accurate. From your forecasts, you can determine just how to fund your expansion.
- **Plan for unexpected events.** The growth of your business will likely be accompanied by risk. It's better to prepare for this as best you

can. One risk you may encounter is business interruption. If your projected cash flow can't help you manage the risk, include saving cash in an emergency fund or getting the correct type of business insurance.

As we said above, having a financial plan is a great move, but it requires actual implementation to see its impact on your business. Implementation includes comparing the actual business results with your projections. These comparisons are particularly crucial when you're still finding your feet at the start of the expansion. Due to the complexity of any business expansion and how much there is to cover, we will discuss this further in the next section.

MANAGING FINANCIAL COMPLEXITY DURING EXPANSION

You've worked hard to stabilize the operations and finances of your business. You feel in your veins that it's time to scale and generate more revenue and profits. While business expansion prospects are exciting, scaling can be challenging—especially financially. You can easily trip and fall if you start scaling your business without the right tools and preparation. This moment is the right time to kick off those preparations and maximize your chances of business scaling success. We will start by showing you what's involved in a business expansion and the challenges you'll likely encounter. Then, we'll tackle what you can do to manage the financial complexity of business scaling.

Understanding a Business Expansion

A business expansion involves taking steps to multiply your company's revenues faster than attracting new expenses and increasing profits. You can achieve this in various ways, such as merging with another business, increasing your product line, extending the size of your production facilities, buying another company, or entering new markets.

Scaling your business can increase your competitiveness, market share, or bargaining power with vendors. However, achievements like these often come with financial management challenges due to the business complexity created. Some of the elements that introduce business complexity include having more employees, more suppliers, more customers, and potentially more locations. When combined, these elements complicate financial management quite a bit.

Your financial management needs to ensure that the existing business keeps generating and maximizing profits and that your expansion efforts are well-funded.

For example, expanding will require attracting and retaining talented staff. This task could be difficult due to the high competition for such workers. To outcompete your peers or larger businesses, you may need to offer more, which will put more strain on your finances. Therefore, it's crucial to have ways to manage the financial complexity created by business scaling.

What to Do to Manage Financial Complexity

Financial management is more crucial than ever when scaling your business. Not only should it use data-driven insights to guide business decision-making, but it should also capture and analyze additional financial data. Doing this helps identify significant business expansion costs and how they contribute to achieving scaling objectives. The financial management function must be robust to cope with the expanding business. You can achieve this function by doing the following:

- **Find out all compliance requirements needed to achieve your business expansion goals.** Scaling a business may include selling your products or services across state or national borders. Compliance applies whether you're offering your products online or offline. Trading across borders brings new compliance requirements such as tax, licensing, and employment. Capital requirements could also govern how much you can transfer across international borders. Move quickly to create banking relationships so that you can execute your expansion strategy at the planned pace.

- **Adjust your financial projections as quickly as possible.** One of your business scaling challenges could be running out of cash. You don't want this to catch you off-guard. Your growth-focused financial plan can help ensure you have the money needed throughout your expansion. However, having a financial plan that stays current as your business expands would be best. This approach is where agile financial forecasting will come in handy. Adjust your projections accordingly as you update your growth-focused financial plan with the actual figures.

- **Automate routine financial management activities.** When expanding your business, you'll likely have someone overseeing your financial management activities. While crunching numbers might be their forte, they can have a greater impact on your expansion if they contribute more to the execution of your business expansion strategy. Automating processes such as budgeting, recordkeeping, and payroll can free them up to help more with your business expansion.

Another crucial strategy for a successful business expansion is having improved cash management processes. This process is so essential when expanding your business that we've dedicated the section below to it.

Enhance Your Cash Management Processes

Business expansion can burn cash quicker than you may have planned. This concern makes it necessary to improve how you manage your business's cash. Here's how to stay on top of your cash flow:

- **Understand your business expansion's cash flow.** Having a cash flow projection for your business expansion isn't enough. You need to understand the actual cash flow as your expansion progresses. For example, you must know how quickly your expansions use cash and adjust your projections. As stated earlier, this analysis allows you to decide where to find cash if you foresee running out at some point.
- **Analyze your cash flow regularly.** Cash flow analysis during business expansion ensures you have the needed cash and helps with decision-

making. For example, when you have ample free cash flow—money available after covering operating expenses and buying major assets— you can invest some of it in highly liquid securities. Remember to use financial ratios related to the cash flow statement for your cash flow analysis.

- **Reduce your sales cycle.** Converting leads into customers quickly means you can invoice quicker and decrease the time between leads and cash coming into the bank. You first need to know how long it takes to turn a lead into a customer during your business's expansion. Once you do, you can think about how you might be able to reduce that period. Meanwhile, ensure you have enough inventory and can deliver products quickly.

While a business expansion is desirable, it exposes your venture to new risks. Knowing these risks ahead of the development allows you to implement mitigation strategies. Here are the risks to be aware of and how to handle them during the expansion of your business:

- **Overextension:** Taking on too much in a short time can jeopardize your business's cash flow and cause burnout. For instance, you may be forced into debt to cover declining cash reserves, increasing your business's expenses. Your business's financial stability will take a hit, and expansion will fail. Proper financial planning will help you avoid overextending your business during expansion.

- **Mismanagement of funds:** It's far better to prevent mismanagement than to try to correct the transgression. It's therefore vital to hire honest finance people. The next thing is to ensure you have administrative controls to quickly catch and address the issue, such as creating finance processes and systems and monitoring your finances regularly.

- **Sudden changes:** A lot can change quickly during your business's expansion. For example, tax laws, environmental regulations, the market, and the economy may change quickly. Prepare your business for the worst with an emergency cash reserve and contingency plans.

What other business expansion risks can impact your company? Do you think you'll be able to deal with them when they arise? How else could you manage the risks mentioned above?

In the final analysis, you can reduce financial complexity during business expansion by having an accurate budget, cash flow projections, a cash flow analysis, and complying with and automating as many of your routine financial management tasks as possible. More importantly, before you expand your business, verify that it and its finances are stable and that you have effective financial management systems (including operating procedures and policies).

While expanding your business is exciting, it's worth ensuring you manage all the risks that come with it. Legal compliance is one of the most powerful ways of ensuring you have effective methods for dealing with risk, which is the primary topic we will discuss in the next chapter.

6

HOW TO STAY ON THE RIGHT SIDE OF THE LAW

Noncompliance can be a quick way to threaten the financial stability of your business and may lead to its death. Consider a 2011 study conducted by the Ponemon Institute that investigated the impact of noncompliance versus compliance on business: They discovered that the cost for noncompliance was 2.65 times more than that of compliance. Six years after the study, noncompliance costs jumped 45% higher and were estimated to keep ballooning (Inspectorio, 2021). For small businesses, increased noncompliance will minimize profits and jeopardize their financial stability. You can stay on the right side of the law if you comply with the many rules and regulations, whether national, state, or local. Read on to learn how to comply, but also a quick note before we get started: Always check with a legal or tax professional about the topics in this chapter.

SAFEGUARDING YOUR BUSINESS

Simply put, your business complies if it adheres to the various government laws and regulations that apply to it. Business compliance is as crucial as your operations and marketing of your products or services. Without it, the survival of your business hangs by a thread. It's essential to take preventative measures to avoid potential legal troubles. There are other benefits you can reap by legally complying, including the following:

- **It improves the growth of your business.**
  There are reasons for the laws and regulations your business has to abide by. Those laws and regulations are often best practices to protect your business and provide a basis for growth. For example, some laws ensure that your business produces quality products or services. Customers who receive a product or service that exceeds their expectations will likely recommend it to their friends, family, and colleagues. In turn, your business gains more customers and increases its revenue. If you

want your business to grow, comply with all applicable laws and regulations.

- **It enhances your business's reputation.**
Imagine how your customers would respond to your business if it were fined for malpractice! You can expect many of them to stop buying from you. If the media picks up your malpractices, they'll spread it far and wide quickly. Your customers can also spread the bad news through social media and online reviews on search engines. Not only will your revenues suffer, but your business's reputation will drop almost overnight in your industry and among the public.

- **It helps your business avoid legal troubles.**
Noncompliance exposes your business to risks such as lawsuits and penalties. One typical example of noncompliance is failure to protect your customers' data. If this data were to fall into the wrong hands, your business could face steep legal fines. With the many laws and regulations governing things like manufacturing facilities, advertising, and the environment, a lawsuit may land on your office desk anytime if you don't comply. The problem for a small business like yours is that a lawsuit can put it out of business in the blink of an eye.

Compliance, therefore, safeguards your business's financial stability.

- **It enhances your business operations.**
Compliance with laws and regulations related to your employees provides a fair, safe, and healthy workplace. Employees who are adequately taken care of will look after your business and its operations, as they will likely feel the need to give back for the excellent treatment they receive. This culture will improve business operations and the quality of your products and services. Additionally, some compliance requirements automatically force you to operate your business effectively. In turn, this stabilizes your business and its finances.

Judging by the advantages above, you have every reason to ensure your business legally complies. Consider hiring a small business legal expert to avoid unturning any legal stone. The initial cost may appear steep, but the benefits that'll accrue to your business will pay for this cost quickly. Of course, hiring a legal expert doesn't mean you shouldn't brush up on your business legal knowledge. The following section will provide some regulations and laws that may apply to your business.

ESSENTIAL LEGAL AND REGULATORY REQUIREMENTS

Business compliance begins when you believe that you have a sound business idea. Running a business without proper documentation is illegal, plain and simple, and you could land in legal trouble. To ensure your business is legal, you need to have the following in place:

- **Business legal structure:** To comply, every new business owner must create a legal structure. There are five common structures: sole proprietorship, partnership, limited liability company (LLC), S corporation, and C corporation. Each business structure has pros and cons.
- **Sole proprietorship:** This is a business structure with one owner. In this structure, you and your business are one entity, meaning you're liable for taxes and liabilities for your venture.
- **Partnership**: In this structure, you share the workload, profits, liability, and taxes with your partner. You can limit your liability by creating a limited liability partnership.
- **LLC:** This business structure protects your personal assets from litigation in numerous

circumstances. You include your business's income in your personal income taxes. You may also pay self-employment tax (which we will discuss shortly).

- **C corporation:** This is ideal if you want to separate your business's assets from yours. Your assets are shielded from your business's liability. C corporations also file their taxes separately. You can earn a salary and dividends from a business structured as a C corporation. Its primary disadvantage is that it's complex to form and operate legally.

- **S corporation:** This legal structure combines some of the features of an LLC with those of a C corporation. It can pass its income directly to its less than 100 shareholders, who take care of their personal taxes. However, it can pay taxes on its passive income. An S corporation is more complex to form and run because it has many requirements, including shareholder meetings.

- **Business name:** After choosing a business structure, you need to register the name of your business. This action makes your business legal and allows you to comply with other laws and regulations. Make sure that your business's name is unique to avoid trademark infringements.

- **Federal tax identification number:** This number, known as an employer identification number (EIN), is required for legally hiring employees and tax-paying purposes.
- **State tax identification number:** If your state charges taxes, you'll need this number. It's up to you to determine if you need a state tax identification number. States like Alaska, South Dakota, and Wyoming don't charge state income taxes. In contrast, states like Hawaii, Maryland, and New York do.
- **Business licenses and permits:** The type of industry your business operates in dictates whether you need business licenses and permits or not. For instance, you'll likely need business licenses and permits if you work in the trucking and cargo haulage space. These permits and licenses may be required at the federal, state, or local level.
- **Business insurance:** While there's a long list of the types of business insurance you can have, make sure you start with the ones required by law. For example, you must have unemployment and disability insurance if you hire employees. For business reasons, you may get business insurance like product liability,

general liability, or commercial property
insurance.

- **Labor laws:** Every business that hires workers
  is required to adhere to applicable labor laws.
  These laws ensure fair compensation, worker
  health and safety, and protect employees' rights.
  Some labor laws apply at the federal level. In
  contrast, others may be required at the state,
  local, regional, or industry level. Find out what
  labor laws apply to your business before you
  operate it.

- **Retention of records:** For audit purposes, your
  business must keep certain documents, such as
  financial and employee records. These records
  can also demonstrate that you've complied with
  the law when challenged or facing a lawsuit.

The list of laws and regulations to comply with is more
than we have provided here. The legal expert we
suggested you hire will be helpful when determining all
the rules and regulations to comply with. When it
comes down to it, you never want to put your business's financial stability, growth, or expansion at legal
risk.

UNDERSTANDING YOUR TAX OBLIGATIONS

Your business is required to pay taxes directly or indirectly through you, depending on its legal structure. Some taxes are charged at the federal level, while others are at state or local levels. As stated earlier, it's vital to comply with the law, and one of the laws pertains to paying taxes. Failure to pay taxes can lead to hefty penalties, jeopardizing your business's financial stability.

If you want your business to be on the right side of the tax laws, pay yours—and pay them on time. Some of the taxes your business may have to pay include the following:

- **Income tax:** This is the tax your business pays from its profit. It varies based on your business's legal structure. C corporations pay 21% of the profits to the federal government. The amount of state taxes you charge varies from region to region. Some states charge progressive taxes, while others levy flat-rate taxes.
- **Self-employment tax:** Almost every small business is required to pay self-employment taxes—taxes that fund Medicare and Social Security. The self-employment tax in 2023 is

15.3%, 12.4% in Social Security and 2.9% in Medicare. You pay these taxes if your business turns a positive profit. The Social Security and Medicare portions apply to the first $160,000 of your net profit. At the same time, the Medicare part comes in if you make $200,000 or more in net profit (Orem, 2023).

- **Payroll taxes:** Do you hire employees? If so, you must pay Social Security and Medicare payroll taxes. Your business should pay 7.25% of its workers' gross paychecks to Social Security and do the same for itself. You may also have to pay unemployment and employee taxes.

- **Sales tax:** Some municipalities and states charge sales taxes on selected goods and services. Your business is tasked with collecting these taxes on behalf of your city or state and passing them on to them.

The taxes your business pays will vary from business to business. For instance, if your company invests in securities like bonds and stocks, it may have to pay capital gains tax and dividends tax. For this reason, consult a tax accountant to thoroughly assess your business to determine what taxes your company should pay.

It's helpful to know how each of the taxes that apply to your business are calculated. We'll explain how to do these calculations using the federal income tax for a C corporation as an example. Suppose you've worked out your business's annual net profit in year X and found it to be $100,000. This figure is your taxable income but not your tax liability. To determine your tax liability, subtract allowable tax deductions, such as state taxes, from your income. Let's say these deductions add up to $13,000 in that year. Your business's adjustable taxable income will be $100,000 minus $13,000, equaling $87,000. Multiplying this figure by 21% (tax rate for C corporations) gives you a tax liability of $18,270.

A business whose tax liability is $500 or more annually should pay estimated taxes annually. You should pay this tax quarterly to the Internal Revenue Service (IRS); its due date is the 15th of the first month following the end of a quarter. For example, the due date is September 15th for the quarter ending August 31st.

Failure to pay taxes or paying late may attract penalties. There are other types of penalties worth knowing about. Some common ones you may incur include the following (TurboTax Expert, 2023):

- **Late payment:** Paying your taxes late may result in a monthly penalty of 0.5% of your tax liability. This amount equals a $50 penalty for every $10,000 you owe.

- **Tax filing inaccuracy:** If a tax audit finds that you've filed your business taxes inaccurately, you may incur a penalty of up to 20% of your total tax liability.
- **Filing your taxes late:** This can attract a penalty totaling 5% of your monthly tax liability. On a $10,000 tax liability, this is a $500 monthly penalty (5% of $10,000 = $500).

Ignoring your tax responsibilities will be unpleasant, as the above tax-related penalties show. Ask your certified accountant for advice if you're unsure what taxes to pay or how to handle them.

Another point to remember is the importance of keeping your financial records. Not only do these records help you evaluate the financial performance of your business, but they also simplify compliance with tax laws. For instance, financial records optimize tax deductibles you can make, support your business income, expenses, and tax credits during tax filing, and simplify tax audits by the IRS. Accurate financial records can help your business maximize profits and operate longer.

ENSURING COMPLIANCE

Knowing the importance of compliance is a good start, but more critical is having strategies to comply and implementing them. Here's what you can do to ensure you legally comply, whether at the federal, state, or local level:

Locate Legal Risks

The first step for complying is identifying and compiling risks in a list. You can find risk in laws, regulations, contracts, and lawsuits. Litigations don't have to be against you as sources of business risks. You can study lawsuits against companies in and outside your industry to spot threats.

Once you've identified risks that apply to your business, list them in a risk register. This register can be a spreadsheet that includes the name of the risk and details about it, such as its sources. At this point, aim to list as many legal risks as possible with no judgment. Note the preliminary likelihood that each risk may occur and what consequences it may bring to your business. Working with a lawyer on this will be especially helpful.

Dissect Each Risk

You can't manage a legal risk effectively if you don't understand it thoroughly. This is where dissecting each risk comes in handy. The outcome of this step is to identify risks that need to be evaluated in the next step.

Analyzing each risk involves refining its likelihood and its consequence on the business. You can look at the factors that lead to the likelihood rating and outcome you identified. For instance, you may look at the likelihood of a tax audit by the IRS and what consequences may result.

Don't worry about precision when rating the likelihood of risks occurring and their consequences. The quality of your risk assessment will improve over time as you iterate it.

Appraise Each Legal Risk

Appraising or evaluating a legal risk means deciding what to do with the risk after you've analyzed it. In this way, you ask if the risk is tolerable or intolerable. If the risk is tolerable, you don't do anything about it. However, if it's unacceptable, there's a need for risk controls so that you can minimize its impact if you can't eliminate it outright. The primary aim of risk appraisal is to make each legal risk tolerable.

Some of the actions you could take to make a risk tolerable include the following:

- Stopping the activity that gives rise to the risk
- Eliminating the root cause of the risk
- Purchasing the right kind of insurance

Generally, there are strategies you can implement to improve your legal compliance. The more of those strategies you implement, the higher the chances that your business will comply. Some of those strategies include the following:

- **Train your personnel.** A knowledgeable staff can save your business from noncompliance. You can enhance the knowledge of your personnel by educating them on laws and regulations that apply to your business. For instance, you can teach them about workplace safety. You can hire a legal expert or professional if you can't do this yourself.
- **Sign contracts you understand.** Whether running an online or offline business, you sign rental leases, phone contracts, and supplier agreements. Make sure you or your employees sign contracts they understand. Consider having a legal expert review all the

arrangements you enter into and advise you before signing.

- **Update yourself on changes in laws and regulations that apply to your business.** This is crucial for staying in compliance. Failure to keep yourself updated on changes in the law or regulations may expose you to risks you thought were covered.

Ensuring compliance by using strategies such as the ones outlined above is crucial. If so, you'll avoid fines, penalties, a tarnished reputation, and a possible prison term. You may have the temptation to think your business can't be caught for noncompliance. Other industries, especially ones with large companies, have failed to comply and have paid vast sums of money.

Let us briefly tell you about one of these companies, which is a reputable airline company. In 2018, this conglomerate fell prey to a cyberattack it failed to pick up for two months. Investigations discovered that the airline company didn't have secure safeguards for the personal information of its more than 400,000 customers. This failure led to a $26 million fine (Neeyamo Editorial Team, 2021). Any business can fall victim to cyberattacks and face the full might of the law. Don't let this happen because you will jeopardize your business's financial stability.

As we conclude this chapter, take a minute to ask yourself if your business complies with all laws and regulations that apply to it. Furthermore, does it have all the mandatory business licenses and permits? Is your business not infringing on any trademarks or patents? Lastly, does your company have an EIN for tax-paying purposes? If you've answered no to any of these questions or know you're not complying in some area, get started with the process of conforming to the law immediately. If you're unsure, seek professional legal advice as soon as possible. Doing so will ensure sound financial management and the stability of your business's finances, especially when overcoming financial mistakes, as discussed in the next chapter.

7

SIDESTEPPING PITFALLS

All kinds of businesses go through their fair share of financial challenges. Unfortunately, economic challenges and mistakes aren't equal. Some can lead to bankruptcy, while others may make you stronger for surviving them. It's impractical to think you'll avoid all financial mistakes, but you can still prepare to handle many of them. After all, mistakes are part and parcel of running a business. Overcoming them makes you and your business stronger.

A case in point is the story of Stephanie Bonnin, a Colombian woman running her business from Bushwick, New York. To keep doing her labor of love (cooking), Bonnin had to be creative when the COVID-19 pandemic came along. Before that, she had hosted traditional Colombian dinners for 16 friends in her living room.

When the pandemic struck, she founded La Tropikitchen to serve Colombian cuisine to the neighborhood. The response shocked her. Within the first week, she acquired 40 regular customers, which grew to 80—and then to 90. Today, she operates her business from a food truck (Munchies, 2020).

When you make mistakes or run into challenges, and you certainly will, you need to be resilient. However, there are some mistakes you can avoid if you learn about them beforehand. In this chapter, we will discuss some of the crucial financial mistakes to sidestep for your business to be profitable and thrive in the long term.

10 COMMON FINANCIAL MANAGEMENT MISTAKES

As much as we can make financial mistakes as entrepreneurs, we can also avoid them by learning from others. For instance, many small businesses need help with cash flow and cash flow management. Learning from them allows you to find cash management strategies that work. Financial crises or other financial challenges that affect small businesses also provide fodder for learning how to stabilize your business's finances. With this in mind, it's a good idea to find out what business financial mistakes are common and avoid them, including the following:

Failing to Create and Maintain a Budget

Creating and maintaining a business budget is simple, yet many small businesses need help. It shouldn't come as a surprise when one of the significant issues small businesses face is a lack of cash or funding. These are the symptoms of a lack of budgeting. How can a company effectively manage its expenses when it doesn't have a spending plan?

Your business needs a budget to avoid overspending and making unnecessary purchases. Your budget shows you what revenues to expect, which helps significantly in planning your spending. Without it, it's easy to forget essential expenses such as renewing business licenses and permits. Buying major items in a month when sales are low is not unusual. With a budget, you can avoid making such mistakes.

It would be best to combine creating a budget with reviewing it to ensure you spend according to plan. Reviews will also help you make accurate future budgets.

Not Creating a Cash Flow Forecast

As stated in Chapter 1 and above, a lack of cash contributes significantly to the failure of small businesses. It would help if you managed cash flow to meet the objectives of your business. The critical part of cash management is cash planning, where a cash flow forecast comes in. Unfortunately, many small businesses deal with cash as and when it comes and goes.

It's vital that when creating a budget, you also develop a cash flow projection. When you have a cash flow forecast, you'll immediately identify periods when you need a cash injection. If you're going to lack cash a few months into the year, you'll have sufficient time to seek solutions. A cash flow forecast will improve your chances of staying in business longer while stabilizing your finances.

Failing to Plan Your Business's Tax Obligations

A business that doesn't pay taxes—or pays them late—puts its financial stability and growth opportunities at risk. You can receive fines or induce penalties, resulting in decreased profits and a bad reputation.

It doesn't matter what kind of business structure you use—sole proprietorship, partnership, LLC, S corporation, or C corporation—you have tax obligations to fulfill. When you run a pass-through business such as a sole proprietorship or partnership, your assets could be at risk if you don't pay taxes.

Tax planning is necessary to ensure you pay all the required taxes. It's a good idea to consider planning your business's taxes once you've created your budget. The projected profit and loss statement has the financial data to plan income and self-employment taxes. If you invest some of your business's profits, you might earn dividends and need to pay dividend tax, which you should plan for.

If you operate in a region that charges sales tax, remember that the money you collect belongs to the government. Be sure you exclude it from your cash and pay it to the proper authority on time.

Mismatching Cash Outlays With Cash Collections

Paying business expenses is a good business practice. Paying these expenses with revenue generated during the same period is recommended. By this, we mean paying March 2023 expenditures with cash generated during the same month. Since this isn't always possible, consider bringing payment of your business expenses as close as possible to cash collections. For instance, if it takes you 30 days to pay business expenses, collect within the same period.

Doing so can have positive impacts on your cash flow. There's no need to repeat what could happen if you dry up your cash.

Failing to Review and Analyze Your Financial Reports

The past doesn't necessarily predict the future. This statement might be true generally, but it falls short regarding business financial management. Your business's past financial performance might not tell you what will happen. Still, it says something about how you manage your business and finances. Suppose you continue operating your business's finances as you do from month to month. In that case, you may run your venture into rocky shores. You may continue making the same mistakes over and over again.

Proper financial management includes reviewing past finances and adjusting your forecasts to mirror reality.

Not Having a Rainy Day Fund

The unexpected can happen, and when it does—like a major customer going bankrupt—it can slap your business right in the face and dry up its cash. When this happens to small businesses like yours, financial stability ceases. Depending on the gravity of the impact of your money, the number of your business's survival days will be less. We understand that you might not have control over whatever emergency pops up, but you can at least prepare for it. If you do a proper risk assessment, you'll know how much cash to have ready for emergencies.

A business can be interrupted by many kinds of emergencies. Some typical ones include the following:

- theft of key equipment
- losing a key employee due to unfortunate events like ill health
- damaged equipment

While business insurance can come in handy when you face some of these emergencies, getting paid from the carrier may take a while. Meanwhile, your business will need to keep running and fulfilling customer orders. You could also get a short-term loan or a line of credit, but these are expensive options. Having your own cash will enable you to ride the rough times cheaply. A rainy day fund can significantly help in such situations, preventing you from using operational cash.

Failing to Maintain Control Over Business Expenses

We can't say this enough: A business that lacks cash dies quicker than one with money. Furthermore, a company that depends on its own cash is better than another that uses external funding. A business must do two things well to use its own money: generate enough revenues and maximize profits. Failure to manage business expenses is a quick way to minimize profits and cash.

The solution is to review and analyze your income statement against your budget. Analyzing the income statement and spotting issues requires comparing your major expenses with your revenue. For example, if COGS is $10,000 and the revenue generated is $25,000, you divide $10,000 by $25,000 to get 0.4. Expressing this number as a percentage gives you 40%. Whether this number is good or not depends on your business and industry. Setting a benchmark to compare against when analyzing your COGS is worthwhile. You can do the same with all the other costs too.

Buying Big Items Early on in Your Business

New business owners often get excited about starting their business. They feel the time has come to be their own boss. Due to a lack of business experience, they buy the best of everything they think they need. For instance, they hire a website designer to build a flashy website, opt for expensive office furniture, purchase software with all the bells and whistles, and recruit talented workers. While all this effort is admirable, the problem is that the business hasn't proven itself to deserve such expenses.

When operations begin, the business owner is shocked to discover that they can barely cover company expenses. After all, they likely fund the business from their personal bank account.

This approach by newbie business owners isn't surprising: the usual cause is a lack of proper financial planning and inexperience. Effective financial planning alone can prevent such mistakes. The key to this planning is creating a budget and justifying each business expense. Also, understand that your business should be self-sufficient as quickly as possible. Starting with huge costs doesn't help. If you've already made such a mistake, consider selling some items and replacing them with things you **need**.

Combining Your Personal and the Business's Money

It may feel natural to mix your business's money with your own. After all, the money your business generates is yours, isn't it? Yes, some of your business's money could be yours if it makes cash profits. When you mix personal money and business cash, how do you separate private money from your company?

There are numerous issues with doing this. First, you complicate compliance with tax laws as one of the requirements is keeping tax-related records. It also makes it hard for accurate bookkeeping and preparation of taxes. Imagine how hard it would be for the IRS to audit your financial records if you mix business and personal financial matters!

Secondly, combining personal and business finances muddles your business financial management. You will have difficulties separating your business's money from your own. As a result, you could mistakenly spend business money on personal matters or vice versa. It'll be challenging to review and analyze your business's expenses. Because of this, you might think your business isn't profitable while it is. It'd be a big mistake to liquidate your business when it's perfectly sustainable!

To avoid making this mistake, open a separate business bank account. This account is where you'll keep all the money that goes to your business and pay expenses from it. Just by doing this, there'll be a trace of all the money your business makes and spends. You'll be able to wave goodbye to all the troubles of figuring out whether your business is profitable. Also, consider paying yourself a salary from your company. This action will remove the temptation to mix your personal and business finance matters.

Cutting Your Marketing Budget

When businesses hit rough times and have to cut expenses, it's not unusual to consider reducing their marketing budget. Some small businesses don't even have a marketing budget to start with. Fiddling with the marketing budget or not having it is a recipe for attracting financial challenges.

Cutting your marketing budget reduces the number of customers you acquire over time. For example, if it costs you $10 to acquire one customer, a budgeting budget of $10,000 will bring in 1,000 customers. Cutting the marketing budget to $8,000 shrinks the number of your customers to 800. Your revenue from your marketing efforts will dwindle by 20% ((1,000 − 800)/1,000 x 100 = 0.2 x 100 = 20%). This mistake, in turn, will decrease the amount of profit dollars you make, which leads to a reduced cash flow.

Instead of cutting your marketing budget, focus on improving your marketing effectiveness. For example, improve your CAC by strengthening your ads, content, and social media posts. If you have to cut business expenses, make it a rule that reducing your marketing budget will be the last resort.

REAL-LIFE EXAMPLES OF BUSINESSES THAT
MADE FINANCIAL MISTAKES AND WHAT
HAPPENED TO THEM

A Business That Failed to Adjust to Changes

Kodak led the photography business during the days of
film-based cameras. It failed to adopt the then-disrup-
tive technology it invented—digital photography—and
faced severe financial troubles. How did this happen?

When Kodak's engineer Steve Sasson presented the
first digital camera to management, he was met with
disapproval. Management didn't see the relevance of
the new technology to Kodak's business. The company
kept this belief even after its extensive market intelligence research in 1981 discovered that digital photography would be the go-to technology in the next
decade. Management's disapproval of adopting disruptive technologies was at odds with how quickly George
Eastman, Kodak's founder, embraced new technologies.
These decisions kept the business alive through a
couple of disruptive technologies.

Instead of transitioning entirely to digital photography,
Kodak employed digital technology to refine film quality. Meanwhile, competitors like Sony, Canon, and
Nikon were going full steam ahead with the development of digital cameras. By 2001, Kodak's sales peaked

before imploding as digital camera sales skyrocketed. The introduction of cellphone cameras turned out to be the final nail in Kodak's coffin. It filed for Chapter 11 bankruptcy in 2012 and emerged in 2013 as a smaller company (Mui, 2012 and Tristan, 2023).

A Book Retailer That Folded When It Was Big

Borders, a company that sold books and music, opened its first physical store in 1971. After four decades, this pioneer of the megastore book business collapsed. Thousands of people were unemployed when Borders went under and shut the doors of almost 400 stores. How could Borders fail when it pioneered a business model that did so well initially?

Like Kodak, Borders was too slow to innovate. When books moved online, it kept on expanding its physical stores. Running a physical store required leasing retail spaces, and such leases ran for one to two decades. While Borders grew its physical footprint, its big competitor built and expanded its online bookstore. When Borders did go online, it sold its books through Amazon.com, helping build Amazon while diluting its brand-building efforts. Another huge mistake Borders made was expanding its CD and DVD business when people could download music online for their MP3 players.

When Borders realized its mistake of handing over its online store's keys to Jeff Bezos, it was already too late —the economy was feeling the heat of the 2008/2009 financial crisis. The decisions and failure to innovate had led Borders into amassing colossal debt. When the financial crisis hit, it became increasingly difficult for the once-thriving business to pay off its debt. It simply didn't have the cash to pay its debt because it hadn't turned a profit since 2006. Inevitably, it filed for bankruptcy in 2011 (Noguchi, 2011; Sanburn, 2011).

How long could your business stay afloat if it failed to profit for two consecutive years? Many won't make it past the first year. It's crucial to watch what happens in your industry to remain profitable. More importantly, you need to move with the times and adjust quickly. These adjustments should be easier for your business as it's a smaller operation, and you can promptly make fast decisions and see their impact.

The Story of Corporate Mismanagement and Theft of Funds

When the Adidas Group shelled out $3.8 billion to purchase Reebok International, little did it know it would soon face challenging times. Seven years after buying Reebok, Adidas discovered that its Indian subsidiary mismanaged funds and business operations. This fraud surfaced when Reebok India lodged a complaint to the police about $100 million in business fraud.

Officials brought two Reebok India executives, an independent director, and other alleged accomplices before the court for their role in the fraud. The issues they had to answer for were falsification of financial information, inventory theft, and swindling of revenues. It took India Adidas' managing director and Reebok India's finance director to report the misdemeanor. The finance director had signed Reebok India's 2012 fiscal year financial statements despite knowing they were false (Dey, 2014; Moneycontrol, 2013; Sinha, 2012).

Adidas took a financial hit for the loss and moved on with business along with Reebok India. After an ownership spanning 15 years, Adidas sold Reebok International to the Authentic Brands Group, a U.S. holding company, for $2.5 billion in 2021 (Dunne, 2022).

Falsification of financial records isn't only a crime in India but in many other countries, including the U.S. Inaccurate financial records influence how much taxes a business has to pay. As a result, falsifying financial records may be considered an illegal strategy to evade tax, which is another crime. If you want your business to thrive long-term, you need to keep accurate financial records and use approved accounting methods when preparing financial statements.

If you've been running your business for a while, review your financial records and make sure they're accurate. Hiring an auditor to review your financial statements and documents might be necessary to help you identify errors. This need to avoid financial mistakes and comply makes innovating your financial management practices necessary. It would be best if you stayed abreast of the changes in regulations, laws, and best practices; for these reasons, our next and final chapter will be crucial.

8

EMBRACING THE FUTURE

The one thing that makes entrepreneurship exciting is innovation—the desire to find unique solutions to current problems. We're sure you want your business to maximize its profits, stay relevant, and keep complying. The fact is innovation isn't a choice—it's a necessity. There are exciting reasons why innovation is crucial. In this chapter, you'll discover what they are, what innovation is, and some examples that demonstrate why you need it in financial management.

STAYING UP-TO-DATE WITH FINANCIAL MANAGEMENT PRACTICES

Technology and financial management trends are changing at lightning speed. Still, they are also enabling your business to stay compliant, so staying up-to-date with these changes is crucial. As we're living in times of information abundance, it is necessary to constantly learn and adapt as quickly as possible. The financial mistakes of companies like Kodak and Borders have shown what can happen when businesses don't keep up with trends, financial management, and otherwise. Read on to discover why financial management needs to be dynamic and to learn the risks you face if you don't keep up with trends.

Financial Management as a Dynamic Business Function

Truly understanding financial management is the first step in learning why staying up-to-date is crucial. Financial management ensures your business effectively plans and controls its financial resources. This awareness means you should identify all factors that can jeopardize this business function. That's why conducting a business risk assessment is necessary to legally comply and ensure you always have the required financial resources.

Financial management isn't a silo business function. Like most business functions, it's open to the influence of technological, political, economic, and regulatory changes. For instance, a regulation that raises the minimum wage immediately increases business expenses with the associated lowering of profits. A business that fails to follow such rules could struggle to pay its debt and thus go out of business.

Historically, businesses went to traditional financial institutions to seek financing in the finance industry. The introduction of the fintech industry is changing this and making funds more accessible, especially to small businesses. For example, instead of applying for funds from a credit union, you could join a crowd-funding platform and raise money quickly. Another significant technological development is how customers pay for products and services. The days of using cash appear numbered, and cashless payments will soon replace it. A business that doesn't adapt to this change will struggle to compete.

Failure to stay current with industry trends, regulations, market changes, and technological advancements puts your business at risk. The bottom line is that either you keep adapting, or your business dies. Some of the methods of staying up-to-date in financial management include doing the following:

178 | DBR PUBLISHING

- attending industry events regularly, perhaps each month, whether online or offline
- employing expandable technology with new features
- building your company as if you want to sell it in the future.

Thinking this way forces you to keep your business fresh and comply with all the regulations. Not doing so means you won't find a buyer, which means your plans will fail. Also, you'll ensure that your business stays on the growth path for you to attract buyers and sell it quickly when it's time to do so.

With the above said, decide how often you'll keep abreast of technological and regulatory changes in your industry. How do you plan to incorporate those changes into your business? As you ponder this question, let's move on to the next section to learn the importance of business innovation.

FINANCIAL MANAGEMENT TOOLS AND TECHNOLOGIES

Every improvement in financial management tools and technologies enhances the success of your business. Adopting the latest financial management tools can give your business the edge it needs. You can see how this kind of technology has evolved over the years to appreciate how beneficial it has become for small businesses.

Before the financial management tools of today, you needed to hire finance professionals to record financial data and prepare statements. The main aim of finance back then was to create financial information to support things like loan applications. Data had to be manually recorded by pen on paper, and professionals did calculations with a calculator. Inevitably, errors propped up more often back then. What was worrying, too, was that companies didn't use the reams of financial data and information collected to serve customers better or improve one's business.

The introduction of computers has led to the creation of spreadsheet-based financial management tools. This improvement reduced the time and effort required to record financial data. However, the user needed to be computer literate to use those systems, which contributed to decreased financial transparency. Automating these systems made them more complex. If there were a problem with the system, it'd take hours, if not days, to find the problem and fix it.

The introduction of cloud-based financial management software addressed issues such as transparency, providing access to live data, simplified financial processes such as reporting, and is easy to use, even for non-accounting users. The cost of such tools has become affordable, making them available to small businesses as much as to large companies.

Financial Management Tools to Consider Using

The technology to better perform financial management is out there. What you need to do is choose the technology that works for you and the needs of your business. The essential financial management tools and technologies you need include cloud-based accounting software, budgeting applications, payroll management software, and digital payment systems. Let's briefly discuss a few of these tools:

Cloud-Based Accounting Software

Cloud accounting software is accounting technology that multiple approved users can access from anywhere there's an internet connection. You can use this software for various tasks, including creating and managing invoices, recording expenses, preparing financial statements, and preparing taxes. Examples of this technology that are good for small businesses include Freshbooks, QuickBooks Online, and Zoho Books.

Cloud-based accounting software comes with advantages and drawbacks:

- **Advantages:** It's secure; there's no need for you to install, maintain, or upgrade the software, and lastly, it offers convenience.
- **Drawbacks:** It requires vigilance to avoid data theft, requires ongoing subscription payments, and works online only.

Budgeting Software

You've learned how crucial a budget is for your business. Instead of using spreadsheets to create and maintain your budget, you can opt for budgeting software. Some cloud accounting applications such as Xero, Freshbooks, Quickbooks Online, and GnuCash have budgeting features, meaning you don't need standalone software. If you prefer a standalone budgeting tool, options include Relay, PlanGuru, and Scoro.

The advantages and drawbacks of budgeting tools include the following:

- **Advantages:** They save time and minimize errors.
- **Drawbacks**: There is an ongoing cost.

Cloud-Based Payroll Management Software

This software automates employee payments, freeing your human resource team to focus on tasks that require personal interventions. It's also valid for accurate employee-related tax payments, such as self-employment taxes, especially when integrated with your accounting system. You can use it to track sick leave, annual leave, and the paying of bonuses. Some payroll management software suitable for small businesses includes Justworks, OnPay, Dominion Payroll, and Patriot Payroll.

Payroll management software, like most technology tools, has benefits and drawbacks, including these:

- **Advantages:** It minimizes human errors, gives you quick access to employee data for analysis, and improves compliance with tax and human resource laws.
- **Drawbacks:** It exposes your data to potential cyberattacks.

Digital Payment Platform

A digital payment platform is a system that allows you to process online payments. It authenticates your customers' payment information and transfers funds from their bank accounts to yours. Some of the common digital payment platforms include PayPal, Payoneer, and Stripe.

The advantages and disadvantages of digital payment platforms include the following:

- **Advantages:** Easy to set up, simplified international transactions, often don't charge subscription fees, and they remove the need for merchant accounts.
- **Drawbacks:** Your account could be frozen if suspected of unusual activity, and you also pay transaction fees.

Financial management tools simplify some of the business tasks you perform. That said, it's crucial to pick the right financial management tools. The key factors when making your choices include the following:

- security
- budget
- features
- flexibility for scaling purposes

Think about your business and decide which financial management tools you need. Search online for such tools and check which one ticks all the boxes of your needs.

THE NEED FOR INNOVATION IN ACHIEVING LONG-TERM FINANCIAL SUCCESS

Innovation in financial management means giving up old-fashioned processes, tools, and strategies for novel ones to maximize profits and ensure long-term stability. You can achieve this open-minded approach by using what we mentioned above to keep your financial management up-to-date. Mind you, it'll be tough to innovate without actively looking for ways to do so. Innovation is the basis of success in life, and so it is in business.

You can look for opportunities to innovate in your competitors and industries. Your customers can also be valuable sources of the need to innovate. For example, you can ask your customers what payment method they prefer. If they tell you they want to use cryptocurrency, move quickly to introduce it.

Another innovation example in financial management is introducing data analytics to determine the success of your financial strategies. Employing data analytics could improve the efficiency at which you use your business's money, especially when combined with other company technologies. Not only does data analytics improve decision-making, but it also helps with fraud detection, which maximizes profits and ensures your company complies with tax laws. Gone will be the days when you have to use multiple systems to gauge the overall performance of your business.

Finding innovative ways to manage your business's finances and performance is crucial. When you face financial challenges or make financial mistakes, look for opportunities to innovate and find far-reaching solutions.

Think about the financial challenges you're facing. Is your business struggling to reach its revenue goals? Does your company pay too much interest on its debt? Is your business still using spreadsheets to keep track of its finances, and it's frustrating to analyze its financial performance? If you've answered yes to these questions, you can innovate now. Go ahead and look for some innovative solutions. If you don't have these kinds of problems, ask others in your industry what financial issues they have and see if you don't have the same problems.

You have no choice but to innovate to stay competitive in the long term. Make innovation one of your business values. Make it a practice of yours—not just a theory. Remember, you'll make many mistakes as you innovate, which requires being in learning mode most of the time.

Dear Reader,

As we arrive at the conclusion of our shared journey through "The Essential Small Business Guide to Financial Management," we are reminded of the incredible potential that lies within each of us. The knowledge and insights gained from these pages are not just lessons; they are stepping stones towards your financial empowerment and entrepreneurial dreams.

Now, we invite you to be a beacon of inspiration for others by sharing your thoughts in an Amazon review. Your words have the power to ignite a spark in fellow entrepreneurs, guiding them through the maze of financial challenges with confidence and resilience.

To leave a review on Amazon:

1. **Grab Your Device:** Open the Amazon app or visit Amazon.com on your computer or mobile device.
2. **Log in:** Sign in to your Amazon account. If you don't have one, you can quickly create an account.
3. **Visit the Review page:** Search for "The Essential Small Business Guide to Financial Management" and navigate to the book's review page. You can also access the review page using your device's camera to scan the QR code below

4. Write Your Review: Share your thoughts, insights, and feedback about the book. We appreciate both positive reviews and constructive criticism—it all helps us grow and serve you better.

5. Submit Your Review: Click 'Submit' to publish your review and make it accessible to others.

Remember, your review is not just a reflection of this book; it's a testament to the potential within every entrepreneur. Your words can encourage others to embrace their financial dreams and chart their own paths to success.

Thank you for your support, and we look forward to hearing your thoughts!

With heartfelt appreciation,
Dr. Bryan Raya
DBR Publishing
Doing Business Right

CONCLUSION

The wonderful world of entrepreneurship can be stressful if your business isn't profitable, complying, or positioned for long-term success. One of the key ways to build a money-making and long-lasting business is by implementing effective financial management. This task involves financial planning and control of your finances.

Financial management starts with creating an accurate business budget and forecasting revenues, expenses, and profits. While you can employ various budgeting methods, a zero-based budget can help keep unnecessary expenditures in check. For any budget to work, periodically tracking actual expenses and comparing them with your budget is critical. Unfortunately, a budget doesn't project cash flows. For this, you need to track and manage cash flows by using your cash flow statement. When it appears you'll need a cash injection, you may want to consider getting credit. That's why credit management and debt management are both essential.

As your business operates, you're going to generate financial data. You can organize this data in the form of financial reports. When analyzed using various financial ratios, you can use these reports for business decision-making. To use financial statements properly, it's essential to understand how to create them, even if you've hired a certified accountant. You'll discover how to maximize profits and cash flows by adequately analyzing your income statement, balance sheet, and cash flow statement.

One of the methods you can use to boost your revenues and profits as well as optimize cash flows is employing effective marketing. This technique begins with creating a marketing strategy that includes business and marketing goals, market and industry research, competitor research, brand messages, and critical performance metrics. For your marketing to work, you need to use the proper marketing channels for your type of audience. Complement this with the appropriate content format using text, audio, or video.

Many entrepreneurs tend to chase efficiency or productivity. That's all good when you know when to drive efficiency and when not to. It's possible to pursue efficiency but not get anywhere due to the efficiency paradox—a concept recognizing you can only go so far with productivity. To avoid it, consider applying effective time management strategies such as prioritizing tasks, scheduling thinking time, and reflecting. Doing so will also help you identify ways to optimize your revenues and profits.

As you build your business, it will reach a point where growth slows down significantly. While your finances may be stable, a lack of development could spell the end of your business sooner or later. It's at times like this that you should consider expanding your company by using methods such as introducing new products or services, merging with another business, or adding a subsidiary. You need to set your growth strategy so that you know why you're expanding, what the risks are, how to mitigate them, and what resources you'll need. Coupled with this, you should create a growth-focused financial plan to stay on top of your cash flow.

Whether expanding your business or not, complying with applicable laws and regulations is vital. This strategy begins with conducting a risk assessment to identify risks, analyze them, and evaluate their impact on your business. More importantly, figure out what to do to mitigate those compliance risks. Some quickest ways to ensure compliance are filing various taxes, paying them on time, and getting the proper business permits and licenses.

It's rare to run a business and not make financial mistakes. Hopefully, you'll only encounter minor errors that you can recover from. However, some mistakes, such as running out of cash, noncompliance, and not having a marketing budget, can land your business in trouble and perhaps even bankruptcy. Be sure you control costs, handle cash carefully, and keep a marketing budget to always look for customers.

The business expansion you learned about will come to pass if you do one thing consistently: innovate. You can apply this innovation to your financial management. For example, adopt modern accounting tools and systems to maximize profits while complying. More importantly, innovation in financial management will help your business last as long as possible.

Successful implementation of what you've learned will not only lead to optimum revenues and maximum profits, but it will also protect your business for long-term survival. Your story could be like that of Kyle LaFond's, the founder of American Providence, a cosmetics company with a 7,000 sq ft manufacturing facility in Blue Mounds, Wisconsin. Before learning about business financial management, LaFond knew nothing about profit margins and managing expenses (University of Wisconsin SBDC, n.d.). Today, he operates and manages his business using proper financial management and has built a profitable and sustainable business. You, too, can follow in his footsteps.

You've embarked on this thrilling journey with us to learn the ins and outs of financial management for small businesses. Now, it's time to put this knowledge into action. Start implementing these strategies today and witness your small business transform into a financially stable, growth-oriented, and expansion-ready venture.

As you implement what you've learned in this guide, be sure to share what you've learned with others. The quickest way to do this is by leaving a positive review so that others can benefit as you did.

REFERENCES

Barton, R. (2022, October 17). *How much should you pay yourself? Here's how to calculate a business owner's salary.* U.S. Chamber of Commerce. https://www.uschamber.com/co/run/finance/how-to-calculate-business-owners-salary

BrightEdge. (n.d.). *How much should I budget for marketing?* https://www.brightedge.com/glossary/define-marketing-budgets

CB Insights. (2021, August 3). *The top 12 reasons startups fail.* https://www.cbinsights.com/research/report/startup-failure-reasons-top/

Dahmen, P., & Rodríguez, E. (2014). Financial literacy and the success of small businesses: An observation from a Small Business Development Center. *Numeracy, 7*(1). https://doi.org/10.5038/1936-4660.7.1.3

Dey, S. (2014, March 4). *Reebok fraud: Two top execs let off.* Business Standard. https://www.business-standard.com/article/companies/reebok-fraud-two-top-execs-let-off-114030401250_1.html

Dunne, B. (2022, March 3). *The new Reebok: After Adidas, what happens now?* Complex. https://www.complex.com/sneakers/a/brendan-dunne/reebok-sold-to-abg-adidas-future-of-brand-shaq

Failory. (n.d.). *What happened to Lumos, India's smart switching company?* https://www.failory.com/cemetery/lumos

Fed Small Business. (2023). 2023 report on employer firms: Findings from the 2022 small business credit survey. *Small Business Credit Survey (SBCS).* https://doi.org/10.55350/sbcs-20230308

Freshbooks. (2021, July 20). *What is debt-to-equity-ratio & how to calculate it?* https://www.freshbooks.com/en-gb/hub/accounting/debt-to-equity-ratio

FullRatio. (n.d.). *Profit margin by industry.* https://fullratio.com/profit-margin-by-industry

Grunden, J. (2020, February 12). *13 tips for building up your business' emergency fund.* Forbes. https://www.forbes.com/sites/forbesfi

nancecouncil/2020/02/12/13-tips-for-building-up-your-business-emergency-fund/?sh=7d805ff32120

Holliday, M. (2020, December 10). *How much of sales or gross revenue should go toward my small business payroll?* Oracle NetSuite. https://www.netsuite.com/portal/resource/articles/financial-manage ment/small-business-payroll-percentage.shtml

Holovach, H. (2023, March 15). *105 email marketing statistics you should know in 2023.* Snovio Labs. https://snov.io/blog/email-marketing-statistics/

Inspectorio. (2021, February 15). *4 hidden costs of non-compliance.* https://inspectorio.com/blog/4-hidden-costs-of-non-compliance

Leone, C. (2019, October 14). *What is a good marketing ROI?* WebStrategies. https://www.webstrategiesinc.com/blog/what-is-a-good-marketing-roi

Moneycontrol. (2013, December 30). *Govt starts prosecution proceedings in Reebok fraud case.* https://www.moneycontrol.com/news/busi ness/companies/govt-starts-prosecution-proceedingsreebok-fraud-case-1372521.html

Mui, C. (2012, January 18). *How Kodak failed.* Forbes. https://www.forbes.com/sites/chunkamui/2012/01/18/how-kodak-failed/?sh=10ad50b76f27

Munchies. (2020, October 6). *Selling Colombian food out of a bedroom window in Brooklyn.* YouTube.com. https://www.youtube.com/watch?v=8dUduiV7UDI

Neeyamo Editorial Team. (2021, April 29). *6 biggest fines recorded for non-compliance.* Neeyamo. https://www.neeyamo.com/blog/6-biggest-fines-recorded-non-compliance

Noguchi, Y. (2011, July 19). *Why Borders failed while Barnes & Noble survived.* NPR. https://www.npr.org/2011/07/19/138514209/why-borders-failed-while-barnes-and-noble-survived

Orem, T. (2023, May 23). *Self-employment tax: What it is, how to calculate it.* NerdWallet. https://www.nerdwallet.com/article/taxes/self-employment-tax

Revenued. (2023). *What is a good credit utilization ratio for your business?*

https://www.revenued.com/articles/business-credit/what-is-a-good-credit-utilization-ratio-for-your-business/

Rodrigue, E. (2023, April 13). *31 influencer marketing stats to know in 2023.* Hubspot. https://blog.hubspot.com/marketing/influencer-marketing-stats

Ruby, D. (2023, July 26). *Social media users in 2023 (global demographics).* Demandsage. https://www.demandsage.com/social-media-users/

Sanburn, J. (2011, July 19). *5 reasons Borders went out of business (and what will take its place).* Time. https://business.time.com/2011/07/19/5-reasons-borders-went-out-of-business-and-what-will-take-its-place/

Sherman, F. (2019, March 5). *What percentage of rent should you pay according to your business' gross income?* Chron. https://smallbusiness.chron.com/percentage-rent-should-pay-according-business-gross-income-71111.html

Sinha, A. (2012, July 16). *SFIO picks holes in Reebok RoC filings.* Financial Express. https://www.financialexpress.com/archive/sfio-picks-holes-in-reebok-roc-filings/974937/

Snitkof, D. (2023, January 23). *The state of small business credit for 2023.* Ocrolus. https://www.ocrolus.com/blog/the-state-of-small-business-credit-for-2023/

Sprout Social. (2023, March 23). *50+ of the most important social media marketing statistics for 2023.* https://sproutsocial.com/insights/social-media-statistics/

Taylor, A. (n.d.). *10 successful small business content marketing campaign examples.* Ruby. https://www.ruby.com/blog/small-business-content-marketing-examples/

Tristan, D. (2023, January 19). *On this date: Kodak declares bankruptcy, 11 years later.* ABC27. https://www.abc27.com/digital-originals/on-this-date-kodak-declares-bankruptcy-10-years-later

TurboTax Expert. (2023, June 26). *Guide to IRS Tax Penalties: How to Avoid or Reduce Them.* Intuit Turbotax. https://turbotax.intuit.com/tax-tips/irs-letters-and-notices/guide-to-irs-tax-penalties-how-to-avoid-or-reduce-them/L7Unetw5B

U.S. BLS. (n.d.). *Table 7. Survival of private sector establishments by opening year.* https://www.bls.gov/bdm/us_age_naics_00_table7.txt

University of Wisconsin SBDC. (n.d.). *American Provenance.* https://sbdc.wisc.edu/about-us/success-stories/american-provenance-2/

Vallone, F. (2021, March 15). *5 inspiring marketing success stories that'll change your brand.* Gamerseo. https://gamerseo.com/blog/marketing-success-stories-a-few-lessons-to-learn

Made in the USA
Las Vegas, NV
23 January 2024

84819610R00121